Domestic Violence and Control

Jan E. Stets, Ph.D.

Domestic Violence and Control

Springer-Verlag
New York Berlin Heidelberg
London Paris Tokyo

Jan E. Stets, Ph.D.
Family Research Laboratory
Horton Social Science Center
University of New Hampshire
Durham, New Hampshire 03824, USA

Library of Congress Cataloging-in-Publication Data
Stets, Jan E.
    Domestic violence and control.
    Bibliography: p.
    Includes index.
    1. Conjugal violence—United States—Psychological
aspects.   2. Wife abuse—United States—Prevention.
I. Title.
HQ809.3.U5S83   1988   362.8′2   87-23555

Typeset by Asco Trade Typesetting Limited, Hong Kong.
Printed and bound by Edwards Brothers Inc., Ann Arbor, Michigan.
Printed in the United States of America.

9 8 7 6 5 4 3 2 1

ISBN 0-387-96628-5 Springer-Verlag New York Berlin Heidelberg
ISBN 3-540-96628-5 Springer-Verlag Berlin Heidelberg New York

Preface

This research began several years ago when an acquaintance, a staff member at a midwestern women's shelter, learned of my interest in domestic violence and approached me about conducting an evaluation of a male batterers program that the shelter was going to implement. Over time, problems in recruiting enough participants, delays in starting the program, and other difficulties arose over the logistics of carrying out that program evaluation. Consequently, I abandoned that research agenda, but with the contacts I made, I refocused my efforts toward obtaining an understanding of the *dynamics* of violence on an interactive level. It was my belief that researchers in domestic violence had not fully captured the interpersonal processes occurring within domestic violence episodes. Over the following several months, I spent many hours talking to perpetrators and victims of violence with the thought that they could aid me in identifying processes indicative of violent interactions. From those lengthy discussions, this book has emerged.

Having had the opportunity to talk, on an intimate level, with men and women involved in domestic violence, I have come to better understand the violence I witnessed and experienced while growing up. It is my hope that those who have ever lived through such violence will find some questions answered in this book. Those who have never lived through such violence may find that the processes that occur within violent episodes are not very different from other interactions, differing only in that one partner responds violently.

This book examines the features and processes that underlie domestic violence incidents between intimates. It is based on approximately 80 hours of in-depth interviews over three months with nine couples involved in violent relationships. As the pages that follow will show, the issue of control emerges as a central theme organizing respondents' thoughts and feelings on the batterer and the violence over time. This book uses the respondents' own talk to illustrate the different patterns of control.

Early in Chapter 1, I provide the reader with a general understanding of what we know about domestic violence. I then indicate how this study

contributes to our understanding of abuse. Three unique features characterize this research, including incorporating both the men's and women's
perspectives, examining the violence over time, and employing the interactionist perspective.

In Chapter 2, I discuss how the present study was carried out. I describe
how the respondents were obtained and how the interviews were conducted, transcribed, coded, and analyzed. Chapter 3 introduces the respondents in this study. Each respondent's background is described, and
the history and nature of their current violent relationship are presented.

In Chapter 4, I discuss the first pattern of control in domestic violence
relationships. I reveal that respondents made sense of the violence they
used or experienced by describing the batterer's emotions and behavior as
in *or* out of control. The batterer's *emotions* are viewed as "out of control"
(thus, impulsive), and their *behavior* is viewed as both "in control" (instrumental) and "out of control" (impulsive).

A social psychological model is used to explain violence in terms of control in Chapter 5. I examine the complex and processual nature of the
violent act in interaction and address the different aspects of the self—that
is, the "I" and "Me" that intrude into the violent act to produce it, control
it, or both. The model resolves competing explanations in the domestic
violence literature (that violence is controlled and instrumental versus
violence is uncontrolled and impulsive) by showing the conditions under
which each is true. Chapter 6 provides detailed evidence from the data on
how the model operates.

This issue of control is also relevant to respondents when describing the
violence over time. This second pattern of control is discussed in Chapter 7.
As I show, repeated acts of violence are understood in terms of the batterer wanting to control the woman's behavior. Becoming nonviolent
over time is accompanied by the batterer avoiding attempted control over
his partner and controlling his emotions and behavior. Chapter 8 discusses
the general implications of this research and future concerns for interactionists.

There are many people who helped make this book possible. I am especially indebted to the men and women who participated in this research.
Their trust in me and openness to share their feelings and experiences permitted me to get into their lives and understand domestic violence from
their perspective. I am also grateful to the officials at a midwestern shelter
for abused women and to male battering counselors who gave me the
opportunity to conduct this research. Their cooperation enabled me to
carry out this research.

Special thanks are also extended to Bill Corsaro, Maureen Pirog-Good,
Donna Eder, and Diane Felmlee who helped me obtain a richer under-
standing of domestic violence. A very special thanks is extended to Peter
Burke who listened to my ideas throughout this research. His support

helped me get through some difficult moments. Finally, I thank those friends who were there when I needed them.

This research was supported by Grant # 86-IJ-CX-67 from the National Institute of Justice, U.S. Department of Justice. Points of view or opinions stated in this book are those of the author and do not necessarily represent the official position or policies of the U.S. Department of Justice.

Jan E. Stets

Contents

1
Understanding Domestic Violence

Domestic violence is a very pervasive and serious social problem in our society. Though there is evidence that within the past 10 years there has been a decrease in husband-to-wife violence, the decrease is small: approximately 1.6 million wives still experience abuse (Straus & Gelles, 1986). This book addresses domestic violence from the points of view of both the assailant *and* the victim. It shows how they make sense of the violence they inflict or receive. *Control* emerges as a central theme organizing their thoughts about the batterer's behavior and emotions: emotions and behavior are in or out of control. Moreover, they also use the notion of *control* in describing the violence over time. For example, repeated acts of violence are understood in terms of the batterer wanting to control the woman's behavior. Control is thus our key to understanding domestic violence.

Battering, abuse, and domestic violence will be used interchangeably throughout this book, and all refer to the physical force used by a man against a woman in a heterosexual relationship that results in physical pain, injury, or both. This definition, unlike other definitions, includes men and women who are involved in a relationship whether or not they are legally married. Though research indicates that violence toward men by women is just as frequent as the other way around (Steinmetz, 1978b; Straus et al., 1980), abuse against women is a graver issue because the physical damage they incur far exceeds what men experience. Generally, men are stronger and can do more physical damage. My focus is on abuse that is directed at women.

This study departs from previous research in domestic violence by examining abuse over time (rather than conducting one-shot interviews) for *couples* involved in violent relationships (rather than just talking to the women). Additionally, it addresses the *dynamics* of violence in interaction. By incorporating the batterer's perspective and identifying the processes that are characteristic of violent relationships over time, we are able to obtain a better understanding of domestic violence.

A Brief Historical Look

Domestic violence has occurred for centuries (Davidson, 1977). From the days of ancient Babylon to the rise and fall of the Roman Empire, to the Middle Ages and its feudal economy, to twentieth century industrial capitalism, men's right to use physical force against women has been lawful and expected (Dobash & Dobash, 1979). Men have been given the right to beat their wives for just about anything: "A woman could be beaten if she behaved 'shamelessly' and caused jealousy, was lazy, unwilling to work in the fields, became drunk, spent too much money, or neglected the house" (Dobash & Dobash 1979, p. 56).

Before the nineteenth century, when a woman married she lost property and personal rights. This had implications for wife-beating. As Langley and Levy (1977) point out:

One of the most bizarre Catch 22 conditions imposed on women by men was the legal concept that when two people married, they became one in the eyes of the law. This prevented a woman from suing her husband—regardless of what he did to her property or her person—because under the law a man and wife were one, and it is impossible to sue yourself. . . it was easy to conclude that a husband couldn't be charged with beating his wife because he and his wife were one. How can you arrest someone for beating himself? (pp. 35–36)

Therefore, women had no legal recourse when their husbands beat them. This supported the patriarchal ideology and the accompanying hierarchical social order that characterized most societies where men were in power economically, legally, and religiously, and women were subject to them. Men's entitlement to domination in social institutions in the wider society also infiltrated the personal realm, that is, in intimate interaction with women.

English common law, upon which American law is based, gave husbands the right to chastise their wives. This right was modified by the nineteenth century "Rule of Thumb," which meant that a husband could beat his wife with a rod no thicker than his thumb (Davidson, 1977; Langley & Levy, 1977; Walker, 1979b). It wasn't until the 1870s that wife-beating became illegal in most states (Davidson, 1977). Unfortunately, wife-beating remained quite common.

By the 1970s, domestic violence reached public awareness as a serious social problem that needed to be stopped. There were two major reasons for the sudden concern of domestic violence: society's intrusion into the family and the feminist movement. Prior to this time, home was viewed as an enduring, loving haven—a protective place from the evils of the world (Moore, 1979). Furthermore, throughout history, "keeping wives in their place" was expected to be a task carried out by husbands in the privacy of their homes. It was not a public matter, and lawmakers preferred not to interfere in domestic matters.

Over time, issues in the private sphere infiltrated the public domain and laws began to be instituted for certain rights and protections of family members. For example, in the nineteenth century, the Married Women's Act was instituted. This enabled married women to retain many of the rights of single women. Married women could now control their own property, have their own earnings through outside employment, enter contracts, sue under their own name, and make their own will.

The 1970s also witnessed the reemergence of the feminist movement. Feminists challenged the patriarchal order and women's second-class status. There was a call for a democratization of power. Furthermore, there was a challenge to the rearing of children in traditional ways where men were taught to be aggressive and dominant and women were taught to be obedient and submissive. The feminist perspective argued that egalitarianism and androgyny should replace the old system of values and social order. As a result, domestic violence was brought to the forefront as a social problem that needed our attention. Because violence in the home was a private matter, it has been difficult to study (Gelles, 1985). When the shelter movement arose in the early 1970s, battered wives in shelters became a source of information for domestic violence studies.

The movement against wife-beating began on an international level in England in 1971, through the pioneering efforts of Erin Pizzey who set up the first refuge for battered women, Chiswick Women's Aid Center (Pizzey, 1977). Several years later, wifebeating received attention in this country. In October, 1974, the Women's Advocates in St. Paul, Minnesota, set up the first American refuge for battered wives and their children (Davidson, 1977). By 1975, The National Organization for Women (NOW) had established a National Task Force on Battered Women (Martin, 1976).

Domestic Violence in Review

Domestic violence should be understood as existing on a continuum of mild to severe forms of abuse (Straus, 1979) with mild abuse occurring more often than more severe abuse (Straus et al., 1980; Straus & Gelles, 1986). Mild abuse includes pushing, grabbing, shoving, or slapping a woman. More severe abuse includes kicking, choking, or beating her, or using a weapon on her. Injury may range from feeling mistreated to experiencing minor to severe physical pain. Physical injury may include bruises, black eyes, burns, broken bones, loss of limbs, or damage to (or loss of) organs.

Abuse is an underreported crime. It is underreported for two reasons: (a) it occurs in the privacy of one's home where there are typically no witnesses aside from family members to detect and report it and (b) though violence is by no means restricted to the lower classes, middle- and upper-class violence is likely to go unreported to the police. First, the wife and/or children may feel apprehensive in reporting abuse for fear of retaliation from the assailant. Or, if it is reported, lawyers may be apprehensive in taking the case to court because of the difficulty in prosecuting the assailant when the testimony is based only on the victim's story (Dellapa, 1977).

Second, lower-class violence is more likely to be on record because the poor and uneducated are more likely than the wealthy and educated to use public social control agencies for help, such as social service agencies, the police, and the courts. Upper- and middle-class individuals are more likely to use and can afford private social resources for aid, such as psychiatrists, psychologists, and marriage counselors (Martin, 1976; Steinmetz, 1978a; Walker, 1979b; Moore, 1979; Straus et al., 1980). Consequently, abuse within the higher social classes is less likely to be reported.

Once abusive behavior begins, it generally does not continue as an everyday occurrence. Instead, it repeats itself in cycles. The battering cycle consists of three distinct phases: (a) tension-building, (b) the explosion or acute battering incident and (c) the calm, loving stage (Walker, 1979b). The tension-building surfaces when a woman notices her partner becoming edgy or reacting negatively to minor frustration (Walker, 1979a). He may cause minor, quick violent episodes. The second phase appears when the heightened tension develops into blind rage that is released through an uncontrollable severe violent incident. The final phase occurs, afterwards, as the man attempts to win back his partner by showering her with gifts and attention.

There are many myths surrounding abuse. The most common ones are that: (a) one or both individuals in the violent relationship are mentally ill (Pagelow, 1981); (b) battered women are masochistic (Gingold, 1976; Schuyler, 1976; Carlson, 1977; Langley & Levy, 1977; Walker, 1979b; Pagelow, 1981); (c) women seek out batterers (Gelles, 1972; Pizzey, 1977; Pagelow, 1981); (d) the battering is justifiable because the woman provoked it (Pizzey, 1977; Walker, 1979b; Pagelow, 1981; Stacey & Shupe, 1983); and (e) drinking causes battering (Gelles, 1972).

In general the myths do not describe the reality of the battering syndrome. If we examine the myths more closely, however, some factors—for example a woman's provocation or a man's drinking behavior—may be more closely related to violence than other factors, such as a woman's masochism or her deliberate attempt to seek out a batterer. Specifically, women may not provoke the violence, but they may influence the conflict that arises. Drinking may not cause battering, but alcohol consumption may increase the severity of violence that is used.

Past research has suggested that the factors related to battering fall under two general areas: (a) background (including childhood experiences and demographic characteristics) and (b) personality factors.[1] With respect

---

[1] A third important factor that has been neglected is the interactive processes of the couple.

to childhood experiences, a generational theory of abuse has been proposed. This theory states that males and females who experience and/or witness violence in childhood are more likely to be in violent relationships in adulthood. Specifically, the males will be abusive and the females will be victims of abuse. This theory has received support in research on battering (Gelles, 1972; Roy, 1977; Star, 1979; Walker, 1979b; Straus et al., 1980; Roy, 1982; Stacey & Shupe, 1983).

Battering also has been shown to be related to a belief in traditional sex roles that are learned in childhood (Moore, 1979). If males are taught to be dominant and aggressive while females are taught to be submissive and passive, such teachings influence violent behavior and victimization in adulthood. If a male child is rewarded for being aggressive and/or observes his father behaving aggressively, and a female child is rewarded for being submissive and/or sees her mother passively accepting male violence, this reinforcement and/or observational learning effects the existence and perpetuation of the perpetrator–victim roles. When a man enters a relationship, he may feel that he is expected to respond aggressively to conflict. When a violent incident occurs, he not only invokes what he has learned but also justifies his abusive behavior in terms of what he has been taught. Likewise, when a woman enters a relationship, she may feel that she is to submit to her partner's will. If violence occurs, she may accept it passively and justify it in terms of deserving it or believing that she is to accept male aggression.

Though battering occurs in all ages, races, religions, incomes, educational levels, and geographic locales, some relationships are more inclined to be violent than others. Battering is more likely to occur among young couples, aged 25–29 (Carlson, 1977; Prescott & Letko, 1977; Straus et al., 1980; Pagelow, 1981; Roy, 1982; Stacey & Shupe, 1983). Some researchers indicate it is more common among blacks (Straus et al., 1980), and others indicate blacks use more severe violence (Stacey & Shupe, 1983).

Keeping in mind that abuse is often not reported in the middle- and upper-classes, men and women in battering relationships tend to have limited education. The women are more likely to be high school dropouts (Gelles, 1972; Star, 1979; Straus et al., 1980; Stacey & Shupe, 1983) and the men, high school graduates (Carlson, 1977; Straus et al., 1980; Stacey & Shupe, 1983). As a result of limited education, the occupation and income of men and women in violent relationships is low (Straus et al., 1980; Roy, 1982; Stacey & Shupe, 1983). Jobs may be meaningless and extrinsically and intrinsically worthless or dissatisfying. The woman may be the scapegoat for the release of negative feelings.

Walker (1979b) provides the most comprehensive list of the personality characteristics of victims and their assailants. Her research indicates that a battered woman has a low self-esteem, believes in traditional male–female sex roles, accepts responsibility for the batterer's actions, uses sex as a way to establish intimacy, and believes no one will be able to help her except herself (Walker, 1979b). The batterer has a similar profile: he, too, has a low self-esteem and believes in stereotypical sex roles. In addition, he blames others for his actions, is pathologically jealous, uses sex as an act of aggression to enhance self-esteem, and does not believe his violent behavior should be viewed negatively (Walker, 1979b).

There are many reasons a woman decides to remain in a battering relationship. Among the rationales she may employ include, "He will change" (Roy, 1977; Moore, 1979); "It is my fault" (Langley & Levy, 1977; Moore, 1979); "I am afraid to leave" (Langley & Levy, 1977; Moore, 1979); "I have no place to go" (Gelles, 1972; Langley & Levy, 1977; Pizzey, 1977; Roy, 1977); "What will happen to the children?" (Langley and Levy, 1977; Stacey & Shupe, 1983); and "I can't make it financially on my own" (Schuyler, 1976; Stacey & Shupe, 1983).

In summary, though statistics reveal that almost two million wives experience abuse yearly, the under reporting of this crime makes that number much higher. Mild forms of abuse are most common. Once abuse occurs, it generally repeats itself in cycles characterized by tension-building, an acute battering incident, and a make-up period. Battering appears to be associated with experiencing and/or witnessing violence in childhood, upholding traditional sex role attitudes and behavior, obtaining a limited education and having a low self-esteem. Many women stay in abusive relationships because they blame themselves, feel that their mate will change, or believe that they cannot manage on their own.

The Focus of This Study

This study goes beyond initial concerns in domestic violence research to examine the neglected third important area (interaction between the couple) by obtaining data over time on violent relationships, utilizing couple data and addressing the dynamics of violence in interaction. First, domestic violence has been examined primarily through interviews with women at one point in time (Bagarozzi & Giddings, 1983). Researchers using this approach depend on retrospective interviews which suffer from respondents' inaccurate recall of past experiences. Obtaining information over time on domestic violence minimizes problems in using retrospective data and encourages a more process oriented approach.

Second, interviews have been conducted largely with female respondents housed in shelters, a reflection of the difficulty of obtaining male batterers as respondents. The direct exclusion of men from research samples is likely to result in a variety of biases of unknown directions and magnitudes. Recently, some researchers in domestic violence have used batterers as respondents (Ptacek, 1985; Rosenbaum, 1986; Hamberger & Hastings, 1986). The inclusion of batterers, however, should not occur to the neglect of the victim's perspective. There is a definite need for research with the *couple* as the focus of analysis (Szinovacz, 1983).

Some researchers have collected data on abuse from husbands and wives from *different* marriages (for example, Straus et al., 1980). This is known as collecting aggregate data. Szinovacz (1983) argues that aggregate data cannot substitute for couple data. He uses couple data (information from husbands and wives from the *same* marriage) and finds response discrepancies between spouses that cannot be captured by aggregate data:

The present data suggest that, at least if sensitive issues are concerned, spouses tend to disagree considerably on the occurrence and frequency of specific behavior. It is also obvious that such response discrepancies are only revealed through couple comparisons and are not necessarily reflected in the aggregate husband–wife data. (pp. 641–642)

One cannot assume that a woman's responses to questions designed to assess the influences of particular background, situational or personality factors on domestic violence reflect the reality of why violence occurs and persists. Relying on the batterer's perspective alone is also inadequate. Furthermore, aggregate data fails to reveal response discrepancies between spouses. Couple data allow more complete evidence on the interactive nature of abuse, why it arises, continues or stops, and how the attitudes and behaviors of both the actors are involved in the violence.

Finally, though many theoretical approaches have been applied to domestic violence (Gelles & Straus, 1979), they have contributed little to an understanding of the dynamics of violence as it exists in interaction. For example, the fact that we know, on a macro level, that domestic violence occurs in all ages, races, religions, and social classes says nothing about why violence occurs in some relationships and not others. If there are some factors that seem to precipitate violent incidents, such as the batterer's low self-esteem (Walker, 1979b), it is unclear why men with low self-esteem in other relationships do not resort to violence. For the most part, domestic violence researchers have neglected the interactional features and processes that occur within those relationships that result in violence. Therefore, we must first analyze violence on a micro level, that is, as part of ongoing interaction.

In this research, it is assumed that domestic violence is embedded in a stream of ongoing, face-to-face interaction. I am interested in understanding how violence is felt and experienced in interaction. Consequently, I employ the symbolic interactionist perspective.[2] Focusing on the interpretive and interactive nature of violence means that the phenomenon is studied from "within." Features of the social structure (such as the position of men relative to women in society) influence violence to the extent that

---

[2] This research takes seriously Denzin's (1984a, 1984b) thesis that domestic violence should be located and understood in interaction. Later, I will discuss how my research departs from Denzin's thesis.

they impinge upon the actor's interpretation of a situation. Let me briefly explain the symbolic interactionist perspective and then show how it can be used to analyze abuse.

The symbolic interactionist perspective is made up of two core components: the view of the self and the view of the world. On the one hand, there is a focus on understanding the person from his or her own perspective. On the other hand, there is an emphasis on how individuals define and interpret not only themselves, but others and situations they experience as well. Interaction forms the backdrop for each of these components. This means that one's self-view and view of the world does not exist in isolation from interaction but rather emerges, becomes solidified or changes as a result of the interactions one experiences.

An interactionist seeks to understand how individuals see themselves and what sorts of claims they make about who they are. Therefore, issues such as self-esteem (whether one feels good or bad; Rosenberg, 1979) identity (who one is; Burke, 1980), and identity salience (the importance of an identity relative to other identities; Stryker, 1980; McCall & Simmons, 1978) become important. Knowing one's self-view is important because individuals act in ways that are consistent with, reinforce, or show their view of themselves. This enables us (and them) to make sense of their behavior.

Individuals come to know themselves, behave in particular ways, and acquired a view of the world through interaction. Interaction ncesssarily implicates at least two people. It is made up of individuals who act and react to their own and the other's behavior.

When individuals enter interaction, it is assumed that they define it by applying names to the situation, themselves, and the other participants, and then they behave according to that defiinition (Stryker, 1980). The definition of the situation gives meaning to their lives. Additionally, it tells them what they can expect of others and what is expected of themselves.

An individual's view of the world is a function of making sense of others and the situation and behaving according to that meaning. Like the self-view, individual's behavior supports or confirms his or her view of the world. As a result, we may understand an individual's behavior on the basis of how he or she perceives the world.

How does the above relate to domestic violence? First, we need examine the self-view (for example, how they feel about themselves) of those who use or receive violence. In order to understand their behavior, we must not only know how they feel about themselves but also how their behavior relates to their view of others. Additionally, we must examine the interaction in which their use or receipt of violence emerged. Specifically, we need to examine how the assailant and victim act and react to each other's behavior. Their actions and reactions are based on how they have defined the situation: that is, how they have labeled the situation in order for it to make sense to them. For example, an assailant may have defined a particular situation in terms of his wife not doing what he wanted her to do, for example, not having dinner cooked when he came home from work. In response, he might get angry and physically injure her. The woman may have defined the situation in terms of needing to care for one of their sick children before starting dinner. She may accept her husband's blows and feel that she deserved it because she did not coordinate her time better.

What is very important is how interactants *interpret* themselves, others, and a violent situation they experience. Their interpretation is important for understanding why they behave as they do. In essence, interactionists address the subjective experience of the actors. They examine how individuals make sense of their experiences. In turn, this sense-making sheds light on how to understand domestic violence as a social phenomena.

Though an analysis of the individual participants, their interactions and perspectives is important for understanding battering, it is important not to neglect larger social structural features of society that affect one's self-view, view of others, and interaction with others. For example, the fact that we live in a society where men learn that aggression is an appropriate response to conflict (while women are taught to be passive and submissive to conflict) and where men more than women assume positions of power, necessarily influences how individuals will feel about themselves and relate to one another. Therefore, features of the macro order will influence features of the micro order.

The symbolic interactionist perspective offers a more complete and better understanding of domestic violence than other theories. Let me explain why this is the case. There are generally three theoretical approaches to battering: (*a*) the intraindividual/psychological; (*b*) social psychological; and (*c*) sociocultural approach (Gelles & Straus, 1979). Under the intraindividual approach are the biological, psychopathology, and alcohol/drug theories. The social psychological approach includes the frustration–aggression, social learning, self-attitude, "Clockwork Orange," exchange, and attribution theories and the symbolic interactionist perspective. Sociocultural theories include the functional, culture of violence, structural, conflict, and resource theories.

There are two problems with intraindividual theories on violence. First, they conceptualize violence on the individual level as opposed to interactive level. Straus (1977) argues that individual characteristics alone can account for only 2%–3% of all battering. Second, there is inconclusive evidence regarding what specific individual characteristics actually influence abuse. For example, alcoholism has not been proven to be a cause of violence. Violence may occur in the absence of alcohol use and alcohol may be used without violence ever resulting (Gelles, 1972). Alcohol may be the excuse rather than the cause for violence (Martin, 1976; Moore, 1979).

There are many shortcomings with social psychological theories that do not examine violence in the way that the symbolic interactionist perspective does. I will address a few of these theories to make my point. The frustration–aggression theory states that frustration influences the instigation to aggression (Dollard et al., 1939). However, everyone who is frustrated does not necessarily aggress. Therefore we need to understand how the self is viewed, which will necessarily lead us to an understanding of why different individuals respond differently to aggression. The symbolic interactionist perspective focuses on this aspect. Moreover, the frustration–aggression theory fails to account for the interactive component of violence.

Learning theorists argue that aggression is acquired through modeling and/or positive reinforcement (Bandura et al., 1961). The learning theory is important in understanding the generational theory of violence. However, this theory cannot explain why violence occurs in relationships where individuals have not experienced or witnessed violence in childhood. For some participants in the present study, witnessing and/or experiencing violence was totally foreign. For example, Kay (one of my respondents) did not consider herself to be abused as a child, yet her husband, Mike, was violent to her. Furthermore, when I asked her in our first interview if there were any relationships prior to Mike's in which men were ever violent to her, she said:

No. Not really. Not that I can think of. I was just totally astounded. I couldn't believe it. I had been grown up in a home where boys don't hit little girls.

Mike, her husband, also indicated that he did not feel he had been abused as a child, had never been violent to a woman in the past, and did not witness violence between his parents while growing up. How can we explain the fact that Mike was violent towards Kay and that Kay allowed it? I argue that we need to delve into the lives of the participants involved in the violence and see how they explain it. Doing this calls for an interactionist perspective. When we do this, we find that the learning theory does not adequately explain people's accounts. This will be shown in later chapters.

The self-attitude theory indicates that individuals low in self-esteem are prone to be violent in an effort to receive attention. In turn, attention aids in the acquisition of a positive self-image. While this theory utilizes one component of the symbolic interactionist perspective (getting at the self-view of individuals), it neglects the other components: the individual's view of the world and the relevance of interaction in violence.

The "Clockwork Orange" theory states that violence occurs when boredom or excessive reciprocity in role relationships prevail. Violence is used to obtain a thrill or create tension in an otherwise "dull" situation. Presumably, low tension is frustrating. Violence is used to raise the tension level. This theory opposes the frustration–aggression theory, which indicates that high tension is frustrating. Like the frustration–aggression theory, it fails to get at the subjective experience of participants involved in violent relationships and neglects the actions and reactions of oneself and the other that influence the emergence of violence.

The sociocultural approaches to violence generally explain violence not in terms of the interactive setting in which it arises, but rather in terms of social structural features that serve to influence and/or support its use. For example, while the functional and cultural theories of violence state that violence primarily occurs because certain subcultures value it (because it maintains, for example, the masculine ideal), the structural approach explains violence not in terms of societal norms but structural strain (e.g., discrimination or unemployment) that influences aggressive behavior. Not only do these theories lack an explanation of middle- and upper-class violence because they assume that violence primarily occurs in the lower strata of society, but more importantly, they neglect the interactive component of battering.

Resource theory (Goode, 1971; O'Brien, 1971; Gelles, 1972; Whitehurst, 1974; Brown, 1980; Hornung et al., 1981) is one of the most popular theories on violence. This theory states that since male superiority is ascribed, if a man's position of power is threatened by the lack of an objectively high status, battering may be used as the "ultimate resource" to control and maintain dominance. Therefore, if a male lacks macro resources (e.g., employment), he will resort to using micro resources (e.g., aggression) to obtain control over another. Men are therefore abusive to women not because particular interactive mechanisms influence the emergence of violence, but because control in the macro order is lost and a way to regain it is through control in the micro order. In this research, domestic violence is located squarely within face-to-face interaction and is viewed as the result of one's self-view and view of the world.

A symbolic interactionist approach has been taken by Denzin. He identifies various important aspects of domestic violence. He does not claim to build a theory of domestic violence, but rather intends to present "points of departure for a critical phenomenology of violent families" (Denzin, 1984a, p. 488). He indicates that at the core of violence is emotionality and the interacting self (Denzin, 1984a; 1984b). The self interacts violently for having lost something, for example, control over oneself or the other (Denzin, 1984a; 1984b). He identifies the structure of violent emotionality and highlights the ways a batterer inflicts his emotions onto the other (Denzin, 1984b). Most importantly, Denzin locates violent conduct squarely within the interactive setting. Violence *emerges* in interaction and is a result of the victim's actions and the batterer's response to those actions. Denzin (1984b) maintains that the violence is given different meanings as it occurs and reoccurs in interaction, is embedded in a situation that has temporarily "gotten out of control" and has consequences for all parties involved.

There are two ways in which my application of symbolic interaction departs from Denzin's work. First, Denzin highlights the uncontrollable nature of violence. In my research, I find from respondents that violence has both uncontrollable *and* controllable elements. Second, Denzin does not address how the phases of the self (the "I" and "Me") relate to the violent act as it unfolds in interaction such that violence may be carried out with or

without control. The features of violence that Denzin identifies are important, and I draw upon them to generate a theory of the dynamics of violence in interaction. Without paying attention to both the controlled and
uncontrolled elements of violent behavior, however, and without putting
violence into the context of the Meadian "act," our understanding of violence is incomplete at best.

To build a theory of the dynamics of violence, I focus on how respondents make sense of the violence. This sense-making is an interpretive process and can be used to gain evidence about the nature of the violent act as
part of an interactive episode. Examining the relationship between interpretations and interaction is in keeping with the symbolic interactionist
tradition (Mead, 1934; Blumer, 1969; Stryker, 1980).

Throughout the interviews, respondents attempted to make sense of the
violence and describe it to me. In their sense-making, they focused on the
batterers' emotions and behavior and described the emotions and behavior
in terms of control. This notion of control is a central feature of the theory
I develop in this book. I focus on how control relates to violence as it
emerges in reflective thought and in interaction over time.

Because control emerges as an important element in my theory, I will
highlight the various ways control has been thought to be related to domestic violence. As mentioned earlier, the resource theory states that when
there is a loss of control in the macro order, micro resources such as violence will be used to obtain control over the other.

The patriarchal explanation of domestic violence (Dobash & Dobash,
1979) is also relevant. Abuse is viewed as a direct result of social and eco-
nomic forces that support a patriarchal social order. Men are accorded
power and control in the social structure. On an interpersonal level, men
get away with battering because of their ascribed power. The resource
theory and patriarchy explanations both link control in the macro order to
control in the micro order. In this research, a different aspect of control
emerges as important. I address how violence is understood in terms of
emotions being out of control and behavior being in *and* out of control at
one point in time and over time.

Though this perspective on control and violence has received little attention, some have employed it. Ptacek (1985) analyzes batterers' reflections
on their violence and finds that the men feel that their emotions are "out of
control" when they are violent. However, he argues that the batterers employ the out-of-control-emotions argument to excuse themselves for
being violent. He shows how the men *use* violence in order to "control"
their partner. Therefore, he highlights the *instrumental* nature of violence.
In this way, Ptacek's work supports the claim made by resource theory and
the patriarchy explanations that violence is used largely to maintain control
over another.

In contrast to Ptacek, Berkowitz (1983) and Denzin (1984b) highlight
the *impulsive* nature of violence. Berkowitz argues that when we study

wife-beating we should view the self as driven by anger, with the result that the batterer acts violently, but in an involuntary manner. Like Berkowitz, Denzin stresses the uncontrollable nature of violence. As I will show later, violence has both uncontrollable and controllable elements, and both of these need to be understood.

Summary

In summary, I use the symbolic interactionist perspective in order to understand the processes and features of violent relationships. I examine violence from the perspective of the individuals. Their interpretations of their violent experiences are important. In addition, I address the interactions in which violence arises, including how respondents act and react to their own and the other's behavior. As I will show, respondents make sense of the violence by invoking the notion of control. I explain how control relates to violence as it emerges in reflective thought and in interaction over time.

2
The Research Study

In this chapter, I discuss the way in which this study was implemented. I explain how the respondents were obtained, how the interviews were conducted, and how the data were transcribed, coded and analyzed. In addition, I explain the relationship between my study and the male batterers program which some of the men were involved in.

Recruitment

Nine couples were recruited for participation in this research from January to July 1985. The couples were first obtained by contacting men who were screened into a male battering group program that was sponsored by a midwestern state shelter for abused women. Nine men went through the screening, were given information about the program and my research, and were encouraged by the coordinators of the male battering program to cooperate in both the program and my research.[1] I called the men after their screening and all agreed to participate in this research. The batterers permitted me to contact their partners to ask them if they would be willing to participate in this research as well. All but one woman, Jane,[2] agreed to be a research participant.

The original agreement with the respondents was to conduct a separate interview with the batterer and his partner soon after the batterer was

---

[1]Only nine men were screened into this program because it was the first time that the program had been instituted at the shelter, and shelter officials and counselors were inexperienced in obtaining recruits. Advertisement for the battering program (through radio announcements and flyers) did not generate as high a response as they had hoped.

[2]Pseudonyms are used throughout when referring to batterers and their partners. Jane claimed that she was no longer involved with Bill, a participant in the male batterers group and this research. Bill felt they still had a relationship. In any case, Jane did not want to participate.

screened into the program, and then interview each of them once a month as the batterers went through the three-month battering program. The batterers would meet once a week with two mental health counselors in a group-oriented therapy session. They would discuss their feelings about their violent behavior and try to learn ways to avoid being violent.

Although all nine men were initially interested and screened into the battering program, some of them did not end up participating. Appendix 1 shows that Ronald, Henry, Larry, and Kevin chose not to enter the group. Ronald had a client whose husband was in the battering group and he decided that there would be a conflict of interest. Larry had already begun individual counseling and decided to continue it. Kevin was taking a night class that conflicted with the batterers' weekly meeting. With the exception of Henry and his partner, who left town several months after my initial interview with them, all the men not in the male batterers group as well as their partners agreed to participate in this research. Fred left the group half way through treatment (see Appendix 1) because he felt his violence was not severe enough to warrant further participation. He also chose not to continue participation in this research.

An interview was conducted with the batterer and his partner soon after he was screened into the program, and then once a month for three months, from approximately July 1985 (the starting and ending dates of the battering program). Fourteen respondents (six couples, and Ann and Bill from different relationships) participated in all four interviews. Because I obtained only one interview from Henry and Jackie and two interviews from Fred, their interviews are excluded in data analysis when the issue of change in behavior, feelings or attitudes are the focus of attention.

Protection and Consent of Respondents

Violence in an intimate relationship is a sensitive and difficult experience for individuals to share. As a result, it was important to clearly state the purpose of my research to the respondents, indicate their right to refuse any questions I asked, stress confidentiality, and emphasize my value-neutral position to their responses. Appendix 2A and 2B (for male participants) and Appendix 3A and 3B (for female participants) present the cover letter and informed consent form mailed to the respondents; they brought the signed informed consent form with them to our first interview. As mentioned, the original understanding with the men was that they would be participating in the male battering program. Thus, the cover letter and informed consent form were written to include this feature. When some men withdrew consent to participate in the battering program, they and their partners still agreed to be interviewed with the knowledge that anonymity and confidentiality would still be secured. In the initial interviews with all the subjects, I reviewed the information presented in the cover letter and answered any questions they had. All of the respondents' names were changed to ensure anonymity. Any reference they made to particular places or people was also changed.

Interview Procedure

I conducted interviews with the couples in order to obtain a better understanding of abuse in intimate relationships. Appendix 4 provides a detailed description of my interview approach. Here, I will briefly summarize the procedure.

Interviews were open-ended, in-depth, and audiotaped. When I asked participants questions about their past or present experiences, they answered in their own words and in as much detail as they chose. I also inquired about their attitudes and feelings concerning their experiences as opposed to merely obtaining information about when or why something happened. Using this in-depth approach enabled me to get to know the respondent better. All interviews were tape recorded so that I could adopt a more conversational style with the respondent, provide a more relaxing atmosphere, and at the same time maintain a record of everything that was said. No one refused to be taped.

I created an interview guide (see Appendix 5) that I brought to the first interview, which served as a reminder of the topics I wanted to cover with each respondent. In the initial interview, I obtained background information, such as whether respondents had witnessed and/or experienced violence in childhood, and whether they had been involved in violence with another person prior to their current partner. Later in the initial interview, I asked questions regarding the respondents' present feelings and attitudes about their current relationship. In subsequent interviews, I brought a second interview guide with me (see Appendix 6) that addressed issues that had the possibility of changing over time, such as respondent's attitude towards the violence, and the form and frequency of violence since our last interview. Both interview guides helped organize and structure the interviews.

Interviews were conducted in a room on a midwestern university campus. They were typically held in the early evening. I arrived early before each interview to set up the tape recorder and review what I wanted to cover. Each interview lasted approximately an hour and a half. In total, about 60 interviews were conducted comprising approximately 80 hours of talk.

As a result of conducting interviews over time, I have collected multiple events, interpretations, perceptions, and feelings about the violence. The data is rich and extensive. In most cases, the unit of analysis is the interactive episode. It is important to remember that previous research has not examined domestic violence on an interactive level. Sometimes I drew upon other data, for example, respondent's feelings and attitudes about the violence, in order to obtain a more complete understanding of the dynamics of violence.

Given that I wanted to examine violence from the perspective of the individuals involved in it, the best procedure to employ was the interview. Certainly, such data could not be collected by studying police records or conducting an experimental study. The sensitive nature of violence precludes it from being studied in its natural setting, the privacy of one's home. Examining violence in public places may not take into account those features that are unique and indicative of domestic violence relationships. Finally, self-administered surveys often result in biased findings if the investigator has predetermined what the respondents will address and how they will respond to the issues that are asked.

Transcription and Coding Procedure

I transcribed each interview prior to meeting with the respondent for the next session. This was done for two reasons. First, I thought it would be easier to transcribe the interview if the experience was still "fresh." Second, because later interviews with each respondent covered, in part, issues from the earlier interview, I wanted a transcript available so that if the respondent did not understand where I had problems with the discussion, I could read part of the transcript and directly state my problem.

The interviews were not transcribed word for word. I deleted false starts, fillers, and repetitions of words or phrases. I felt that it would be easier to analyze the interviews without them because I was more interested in the content of the talk than the style of presentation. Later, if I felt that it was important to know how something was said, I could always return to the original tapes.

I did not change the content of how something was said. For example, when Ronald said:

Because, I'm not in a relationship it a lot easier to just sublimate that if something else cause I just don't get in fights. I don't ever go to a bar and get drunk and get into a fight or anything like that. So, if I can figure out whatever makes me click, then I can take care of it and all areas. But right now, it seems to have click more in a relationship.

I did not change it to:

If I was not in a relationship, it would be a lot easier to sublimate my violence because it seems to occur more in a relationship. I just don't get into fights with others outside of a relationship. If I can understand my violent behavior, then I can control it in whatever area of my life it occurs.

Though this second transcription is easier to understand, I did not think it was an appropriate path to take for two reasons. First, I would lose a part of Ronald's personality if I rephrased his thoughts; I thought that keeping as much of his character as possible in the transcripts would be helpful in later analyzing his interpretations and feelings on things. Second, I may have erred in my rephrasing, or I may have rephrased it differently at a different time. If the transcript remained true to his way of expressing himself, I would limit my biasing effect.

The interviews were transcribed by directly typing each tape recorded conversation into a computer file. This facilitated the coding and analysis of the data. After all the transcript files were created, copies were printed and coded. The coding procedure is discussed in Appendix 7.

Analysis

The method of analysis used in this research is abduction, which combines both induction and deduction. Induction uses a "bottom–up" method of analysis wherein particular patterns or themes embedded in the data are identified, and hypotheses are then generated to account for the patterns. Strict deduction uses a "top–down" method of analysis. Here, specific sociological theories or hypotheses are tested to see if they are adequately confirmed by the data. A looser form of deduction involves using a theory or perspective as a guide for interpreting and understanding the data. In this form, the theory or perspective is not strictly tested.

In this research, induction was first carried out by examining all of the data and identifying stable patterns or themes. The most pervasive theme to appear in the approximately 80 hours of talk was the notion of control. After identifying this theme, I returned to the data and examined the various ways in which the idea of control was expressed.

The symbolic interactionist perspective was used to guide me in the reanalysis of the data. For example, symbolic interactionists view as particularly relevant to social investigations such issues as the meaning objects have for individuals, individuals interpretations of themselves, others, and situations, and concerns such as the self and process of interaction. These issues served as reference points from which to view the ways control may have been operating. Consequently, when re-examining the data, concerns of symbolic interactionists were invoked to understand how control was revealed. The investigative process continued in a constant movement between the data and symbolic interactionist principles in an effort to interpret the dynamics of domestic violence. Let me highlight, here, how control was implicated in domestic violent relationships.

Among symbolic interactionists, in interaction, interpretations of: (*a*) one's own covert experiences, and (*b*) one's own or the other's overt actions arise in order to make sense of a situation. The process of interpretation entails the use of meaning. Specifically, the process involves two steps:

(*a*) pointing out to oneself that objects (things) have meanings, and (*b*) selecting, checking, suspending, and transforming meanings in lieu of one's present situation (Blumer, 1969).

Blumer (1969) outlines four steps in the constitution of objects: (*a*) we become aware of some "thing" in our environment and focus our attention on it; (*b*) we assess it and try to figure out what the "thing" is; (*c*) we symbolically designate the "thing"—that is, we give it a name thereby rendering it meaningful; and (*d*) we act on the basis of the meaning. Objects are anything that can be indicated, referred to, or pointed out. The nature of an object is the meaning that it has for oneself.

The data in this research reveal that the "thing" the respondents focus on and thereby name (rendering it meaningful) is the aspect of control. As objects have different meanings for different people, however, it is also the case that objects have different types of meaning for a single individual. As Blumer pointed out, meanings can be modified according to the situation. Control as an object assumed different types of meaning depending upon the context in which it was used. When respondents discussed their view of self or other and change in self or other, the notion of control was invoked in an attempt to understand the violence. Moreover, when examining the violence over time, the aspect of control was again invoked in order to make sense of reoccurring violence or an end to violence.

Symbolic interactionists have focused on various features related to the self, including self-concept and self-esteem (Rosenberg, 1979), identity (Stryker, 1980), and roles (Turner, 1978). How control relates to the self, however, is a relatively unexplored area in symbolic interaction. In this study, it will be shown that the aspect of control is intimately linked to the self.

This Research and the Male Batterers Program

This research remained separate from the male battering program. This was primarily because the counselors did not agree to let me observe male battering group sessions. They also did not permit me to video- or audio-tape group sessions. They felt that my presence or the presence of technical equipment might make the batterers defensive in group sessions. Because this was the first time that the mental health counselors had ever led a batterers group, they were cautious and avoided what they viewed as potential problems in dealing with the men. They wanted the men to feel comfortable, open, and honest about their feelings in group sessions, and they did not want to risk such openness by my intrusion into the program. I respected the counselors' decision.

Though the counselors were fully informed of my research before they started the battering program, I worked independently after they started the group sessions. I initially contacted the men and their partners after the counselors had met with the batterers, and it was my responsibility to keep in touch with the couples and meet with them for further interviews. I rarely talked to the counselors after the sessions got underway. They felt that such an arrangement would be easier for them in dealing with the batterers and their problems with their violence.

The batterers who were participating in the battering program were open with questions I asked about the group. However, I was careful not to alienate any of them by delving too deeply into what occurred in those sessions. In part, they had been told by the counselors that they were to keep confidential group sessions. I did not want to violate their confidentiality and put the batterers in an uncomfortable position.

Before the group session began, the counselors informed me of the program format. The first four weeks would focus on avoiding violent behavior. The second four weeks would emphasize avoiding feelings of anger that might influence violent outbursts. The last four weeks concentrated on changes in the batterer's attitude about the appropriateness of violence. The batterers typically kept me informed about where they were in the program and whether or not they thought the weekly sessions were helpful.

After the program ended in mid-October and I had completed all of my interviews with the respondents, I met with one of the counselors to discuss his reflections on the battering program and to inform him that my research would end. He indicated that the batterers did not speak negatively about my interviews with them at any time throughout the program. He felt that my research remained separate from the group sessions and he was pleased with that.

3
Participants

Demography of Respondents

Appendices 8A and 8B present descriptive data on the participants. The majority of respondents were in their late twenties. All but two men were white. There is a slight tendency for the respondents to have no religion and to have never been previously married. The data on education reveals that the majority of respondents had at least some college education. Thirty-three percent were employed full time, 39% worked on a part-time basis, and 28% were unemployed. The combined income of the couples was relatively low, with 78% of them earning less than $14,000 a year.

Appendix 9 shows the type of treatment respondents participated in during the time I interviewed them. As indicated in the table, some respondents participated in only one type of treatment and participation was brief (e.g., Ronald, Henry, Jackie, Kevin, and Lisa). Others participated in several different types of treatment and participation was longer (e.g., Mike, Larry, Terri, Doug, and Bill).

Whether or not the couples remained together or apart changed over time. I first interviewed Ronald and Kathy in January 1985. The following month, Kathy ended her relationship with Ronald, but she did not move out of his place until mid-May. Henry and Jackie ended their relationship in January 1985. It was not until several months later that I interviewed the two of them. I first interviewed Fred and Ann in May; in June, they divorced. Mike and Kay separated in early March; my first interviews with them were in June; by late November 1985, they were back together. In June, I first interviewed Larry and Terri. In July, Larry moved out; he moved back with Terri in mid-September. Doug and Wendy were living together in June when I first interviewed each of them. In August, Wendy moved out and ended her relationship with Doug. Kevin left Lisa in the beginning of June when I first interviewed them; in July, Kevin moved back with Lisa. In July, I first interviewed Bill; he moved in with Jane in mid-August and moved out a week later. When I first interviewed Nancy and Frank in July, they were living together; Nancy moved out at the beginning of August, and a week later, moved back with Frank.

Participants

The following is a brief description of each of the participants as an individual and as part of a couple. The narrations are obtained from questions I asked them in the initial interview. The summaries are chronological and factual and include several areas. First, I describe the participants' family and educational background, work experience, and experience of violence when young and while dating. Second, I present a general history of how the participants' relationships developed. This includes when the individuals started dating; whether the dating led to cohabitation or marriage; how they got along, how they felt about each other, and whether this changed over time.

In order to understand the nature of the violence within the relationships, I indicate when the violence began and whether its form and frequency changed over time. The cause of violent incidents and how the individuals felt about the violence is also addressed. Finally, I indicate whether the relationship remained intact. This index captures how the violence affected the relationship over time.

COUPLE 1: RONALD AND KATHY

Ronald was 27 years old and white; he was born in Illinois. He had attended the University of Illinois. After taking his degree in education, he traveled west. He had settled for a time in Colorado and had found a job helping the physically handicapped; he had had experience working with the disabled in college. In June 1983, he returned to the Midwest and set up residence in a small town to be near his best friend from high school. The last time I met with Ronald (October 1985), he planned to return to Colorado in the summer of 1986 with another high school friend. He was working full time at a job placement office during the time I interviewed him.

Ronald has an older brother, younger sister, and younger brother. He identifies most strongly with his younger brother, who, like himself, he sees as "somewhat removed from the family." In early interviews, Ronald revealed that he had never felt close to his father while growing up. He claimed that he could never trust his father to listen to him when he needed someone to talk to. In later interviews, Ronald shared how his individual counseling with a psychologist enabled him to accept his father for who he was.

Ronald had been close to his mother when he was young, but his adolescent years had strained their relationship. As a teenager he had started using marijuana, and he had felt that his mother could not understand the life-style of his generation. There was a breakdown in communication. He did not feel as close to his mother since adolescence, but he claimed there was mutual respect between them and, unlike before, an ability to talk to one another.

Ronald mentioned that his father had hit him frequently when he was young. It was not until recently that he interpreted this as his dad beating him a lot. He had a discussion with a friend one day about it and his friend enabled Ronald to reinterpret his experiences with his father as rather violent. Ronald said that previously he had defined beatings on the basis of the consequences they had: that is whether or not they resulted in bruises. Then, through his friend, he realized that being struck many times by his father exemplified experiencing violence in childhood, even though no overt injury resulted. Though Ronald claims to have experienced violence, he said he had never witnessed violence between his parents.

Before his relationship with Kathy, Ronald had behaved violently towards others on two different occasions. In college, towards the end of a relationship with a woman, he had hit her on the side of the head and knocked her down. Another time, as that relationship was ending, he had hit a male friend in the arm after an argument regarding this woman.

Kathy was 26 years old and white; she grew up in Ohio. She had attended Ohio University and obtained her bachelor's degree in psychology. She has been somewhat of a political activist in college. She had entered a Marxist group in an attempt to get involved with a man she was interested in. Later on, she had become involved in the feminist movement and was active in various women's groups around campus.

Kathy had decided to go to graduate school at the University of Colorado to study clinical psychology. Once there, she decided she was tired of school, so she picked up a part-time job at a small restaurant. Eventually, she returned to the midwest. During the time in which Kathy and I met, she was working full time in a grocery store.

Kathy had grown up in a Jewish family. She had two older sisters and claimed to have a good relationship with both of them. She claimed that her parents had always yelled at each other and her father, having a bad temper, would always yell at the kids. Despite the arguments between her parents and with the children, Kathy had never experienced or witnessed violence in childhood. Additionally, she had never experienced violence in relationships prior to Ronald.

Ronald and Kathy met in the late spring of 1983, in Colorado. Kathy wanted to do some traveling and then return to the Midwest where she had friends she wanted to visit. Kathy advertised for a rider to help share her expenses for the trip. Ronald answered the ad. Upon meeting, they spent the day and night together. Kathy claims that although Ronald immediately fell in love with her, it took her several weeks to grow to even like him. When she decided she liked him, she agreed to have him as a rider, especially since no one else had answered her ad. They spent the month of May making plans for the trip.

One night, a week before they left, they were sleeping and Kathy suddenly heard Ronald scream some foul words in his sleep. Kathy tried to wake him but was not successful. Frightened, she went to another room to sleep. Soon afterwards, Ronald came in and threw a pillow at her because he thought she had left the house. Kathy cites this incident as the beginning of the violence.

One night during the first week of their trip, Kathy was asleep and Ronald got up and punched her in the arm. Both of them indicated that they were not clear why that had happened. After the incident, Kathy decided that they would travel to the house of one of her friends in Iowa where she felt she could be safe. Ronald agreed to seek counseling before they continued their trip.

They lived in Iowa for about a month. Kathy stayed at her friend's house and Ronald rented a room on a man's farm. Ronald met with several different counselors. Kathy went to couples counseling with Ronald for about two weeks. They started to work things out. They made an agreement not to be sexually intimate for the remainder of the trip and continued with their travelling. They both claimed that this agreement put a strain on their relationship. They verbally fought with each other for most of the remainder of the trip.

They eventually arrived at the town where Ronald's best friend from high school was living. They agreed that they would stay with him for a few days and then Kathy would take Ronald to his hometown. One night during their stay, they got into a fight about Ronald's friends (Kathy had heard that Ronald's best friend's girlfriend did not like her) and in the midst of the fighting, Ronald kicked Kathy. They agreed to immediately drive to Ronald's hometown where Kathy would drop him off and leave him. However, Kathy stayed the weekened at his home. They discussed their relationship and agreed that they just needed time away from each other. They decided that Ronald would travel with her to Michigan where he could help her set up residence. Once she found a place, he left town and returned to his best friend's residence.

Kathy lived in Michigan for six months (October 1983 to January 1984). She kept in contact with Ronald and would often visit him on the weekends. Because they were getting along much better, Ronald asked her to move to the town where he was living. He wanted to try the relationship again. She agreed, and in February she moved. She found a place of her own and started working as a research assistant at a major university.

From February to June, problems started arising in the relationship again. Arguments became more frequent, and during those arguments it became quite common for Ronald to hit things (he once put a hole in Kathy's apartment wall) and throw things. Sometimes he threw things at Kathy: once during an argument while he was cooking, he threw a hot pan at her.

In June, Kathy decided to travel south for a couple of months with a woman friend. She felt that she needed time away from Ronald and she wanted to do some more traveling. She traveled for only a month because she and her friend were not getting along. Kathy said that this was partly because she was unhappy about her relationship with Ronald, and she had taken this unhappiness out on her friend. She returned in early July, and Ronald told her that he was not ready to see her again. He needed more time alone. They agreed that it would be best if each of them started dating other people.

Kathy began dating a man named Philip and soon moved in with him. She and Ronald would see each other sometimes, and one night while they were together Philip came up in their conversation. In the midst of the conversation, Ronald became very angry at Kathy regarding her relationship with Philip. The conversation went from bad to worse and resulted in him kicking her in the chest, throwing her on the floor, and slamming her head against the floor. Kathy immediately left his house and started walking home. Ronald followed her. Kathy told Ronald that she was going to go to the police. Ronald said that there was nothing the police could do because there were no physical signs that she had been injured. Kathy believed he was right and never went to the police.

A couple of weeks later, Kathy left Philip because she felt that they were incapable of having anything more than a friendship. In September 1984, she moved in with Ronald because they had been seeing each other again and he had an extra room in his house. They again started having problems with their relationship. Once again, the frequency of arguments increased. In late September, they had an argument over Ronald's friends. Kathy felt that she was being neglected—that Ronald was spending too much time with his friends and not enough time with her. Ronald got angry during the discussion and hit her. For the first time, Kathy hit him back. She said that there were two reasons for her reaction. First, she had been taking judo at the time and had been learning how to defend herself. Second, she was beginning to feel that it was unfair that Ronald could get away with hurting her without her being able to hurt him in response. After she hit him, she immediately ran to her bedroom and cried. He came in soon afterwards, and they started fighting again. This time, Ronald pushed her and knocked her head up against the wall and started choking her. He eventually let go of her.

Both Ronald and Kathy note that violent incidents became more frequent after September. It is already clear that they became more severe. However, the next major incident did not occur until January 1985. A week after I met with Ronald, I interviewed Kathy. She indicated that they had an argument (again, over the fact that Ronald was not spending enough time with her) and he started choking her. She pulled away from him and then ran into the kitchen. He followed her and started breaking glasses and dishes all over the kitchen. Kathy then ran into her bedroom and locked the door.

In February, Kathy decided to end things with Ronald. She felt that the relationship could not continue due to the frequent verbal fights and acts of violence. She started dating other men but continued to live in the same house with Ronald. However, she and a male friend (who also lived in the house) decided that they would look for another place together. They did not find a place until May, and between February and May, Ronald and Kathy fought with each other continuously. Kathy noted that there were at least two violent incidents every month. After a time, Kathy refused to be at home with Ronald unless there was another housemate present.

Kathy started dating a man named David, and the last time I talked with her she was still seeing him. Ronald was not dating anyone seriously. Ronald and Kathy did not communicate with each after Kathy left in May.

It appeared that Ronald and Kathy had different expectations about what they wanted out of a relationship. Kathy felt that Ronald spent too much time with his friends and not enough time with her. Ronald felt that Kathy demanded too much of his free time. This seemed to be what caused many violent episodes. In addition, Ronald became jealous every time Kathy started dating other men. Not only was he upset about her relationship with Philip, but also her relationship with David. When she started seeing David, Kathy claims that he became more abusive and even vulgar. On two separate occasions, he masturbated in front of her against her will.

As Ronald looked back on the violence, he never understood why she did not leave earlier. He implied that part of the reason it continued was because she stayed, especially towards the end. He noted that much of the violence was due to the fact that he took too much responsibility for her life. When she complained of being unhappy, he felt frustrated, powerless, and out of control. He responded by behaving violently. Kathy believed that she deserved the violence because she was not ready to have someone love her. In fact, she claimed that she would take measures to have him harm her because she could not accept someone loving her. Yet, at the same time, she wanted his love. This view changed very little in future interviews with her. Kathy also felt, however, that in many ways she challenged Ronald's belief about who he was. She felt that he always put on a different face to different people so that he could be accepted by all his friends. Kathy believed that she confronted him with the various personalities that he was putting on and taking off depending on who he was with, and that this threatened Ronald. In response to this threat, he behaved violently.

COUPLE 2: HENRY AND JACKIE

Henry was 25 years old and white, he was originally from Pennsylvania. He had completed his undergraduate work at Cornell University. After college, Henry had entered law school at the University of Pennsylvania. He completed his degree in May 1985 and moved to Chicago to work as a lawyer for a corporation.

Henry grew up in a Catholic family, with three older brothers, one older sister, and one younger brother. Henry indicated that his father had been a "pretty stern disciplinarian," but he believed that his older brothers had gotten the worst of it. He said that there had been no violence between his parents while growing up. They got along very well.

In the eyes of his siblings, Henry had been the spoiled member of the family. He was the one who received his father's name. Henry traced his special treatment to when he was about a week old, when he had gotten whooping cough and nearly died. He thought that perhaps his mother had vowed that if he lived, he would be marked with special care. His mother had always come to his aid when it appeared that his father was a little too physical with Henry.

Henry admits that he had often been verbally abusive to his mother during adolescence, but she never told his father. He claimed that he had grown out of that and had come to admire and accept her. He assessed his relationship with his parents now as quite good. He felt that he could talk to them, which is something he could not do when he was young.

Henry had gone through two serious relationships in college but said he had never hit a woman before. When I talked to him, he was concerned about his ability to love a woman, feeling that he was not ready to love yet. He revealed that one of his serious relationships in college ended abruptly because he had gotten "turned off" by the woman quite suddenly. He felt a similar experience occurred with Jackie but that he did not end the relationship soon enough. He said that he did not know whether he could trust his feelings for another woman, wondering whether those emotions he felt would be long lasting. He felt he had not grown up enough to be involved in a relationship.

Jackie was 20 years old and white; she grew up in Florida. She had gone to the University of Washington. In her senior year, she married a man she had been living with for three years. After college, she had obtained a law degree from the University of Chicago. She then moved to Nevada for a year and had worked as a lawyer. She later moved to the Midwest, and when I met her she was a public defender for a small midwestern town. At about this same time, she divorced. Her plans were to return to Nevada in July, 1985.

Jackie was the youngest in a Methodist family of four girls. She indicated that she had come from a fairly physical family. She remembered having many physical fights with her sisters. She had been spanked a lot by her parents and remembered that when she got older, she would grab her mother's arms to stop her from hitting her.

Despite the fact that Jackie had experienced violence when she was young, she had never witnessed violence between her parents. The concept of a man slapping a woman was foreign to her, she said; the fact that a man might literally sit on a woman and beat her was something she felt was horrible and had never experienced before her relationship with Henry.

Jackie recalled several experiences of violence in relationships prior to

Henry. She said, however, that she was the person who initiated the violence. The violent episodes, in which she would hit the men, had occurred once with her high school boyfriend, several times with her ex-husband while they were married, and once with a man she dated soon after her divorce.

Henry and Jackie met at a law student's party in August 1983. They immediately were attracted to one another. Jackie was already involved with another man (and separated from her husband) so she decided not to go out with Henry. In September, the man that she was involved with left town, and Jackie started dating Henry. They quickly fell in love.

From the fall of 1983 till the spring of 1984, things went well. Jackie said that in January and February 1984, however, Henry started showing signs of "weird behavior," especially when he was drunk. For example, one night they were at a bar and Henry got upset because he was lusting after a waitress, but knew that he could not act on his feelings because Jackie was with him. When they got home, Henry, in response to his frustration, became violent and started breaking lamps and ripping down pictures from his wall.

In early spring, he started becoming verbally abusive to Jackie. One night they were at a bar and Henry started yelling at her in the bar because she was conversing with another man. That summer, Henry moved to Madison to work as an intern for a law firm. Jackie visited him every weekend but noted that they would inevitably get into an argument every Friday night.

Both Henry and Jackie cite the first violent incident as occurring that summer. In April, the man that Jackie had been dating prior to Henry came to town, and they spent the night together. Jackie had never told Henry. In June, she felt that she needed to be honest with him and tell him what happened. Henry responded by throwing her on the bed and attempting to choke her.

The next incident occurred in May. Henry had dined with a woman, which resulted in getting an account from her for the firm he was working for. Although Henry told Jackie the date was a business meeting, he later told me that he was really "wanting to pick her up." In any case, Jackie found out about the date quite by accident from a friend. She knew who the woman was and got upset because she had previously met her and did not like her. She immediately drove up to Madison, stormed into Henry's apartment, and started yelling at him for what she had found out. She slapped him about three or four times, and he responded by backhanding her in the mouth. It resulted in a black lip.

They decided to take a vacation the following month. They felt that they needed time to themselves, given the distance and job stress they experienced in the prior months. They traveled to Washington, D.C., and while they were there, Jackie called a male friend who lived in the area. Henry had previously told Jackie that he did not want her communicating with him. When Jackie got off the phone, Henry started slapping her in the face because she went against his wishes.

Sexual problems arose as verbal and physical fights became an aspect of their relationship. Jackie frequently mentioned that Henry began to withdraw sexually as the relationship began to sour. Henry noted his lack of interest in sex with Jackie as the arguments and physical violence increased. The sexual problems that they encountered bothered both of them, because early in their relationship they enjoyed sex very much and saw it as a central aspect of their relationship.

In late November, the next incident occurred. Jackie had told Henry that she was going to spend Christmas vacation skiing with an old boyfriend. Henry was furious with her decision and pushed her around all night. Jackie noted that he really wanted to fight her. That night, they went out with some of Jackie's friends. The conversation with her friends turned to a discussion about a man that Jackie used to date; Henry got upset. On the way home, Henry was verbally abusive to Jackie. He swore at her and insulted her. When they drove up to Jackie's house, Jackie was upset and punched Henry in the arm. Henry responded by hitting her in the head and shoulders, pulling her hair, and pounding her head against the door and dash board. He stopped after Jackie started to scream. They went inside, and both started to cry.

The final incident happened a couple of weeks later. Jackie decided that she was going to start dating other men because her relationship with Henry was not working. She went out on a date one night. She had made plans to get together with Henry later that night. The earlier date took longer than she had anticipated and Henry got upset because she was late to meet him. They ended up in an argument that night because Jackie wanted to talk about their relationship and Henry did not. Henry left her house. Jackie went over to his house to discuss the matter with him further. Henry did not want to see her. Several times he asked her to leave; she refused. Things went from bad to worse and Henry ended up beating her. The beating resulted in bruises all over her body, a black and blue lip, and a torn pectoral muscle. The police were called to the scene but were driven away by Henry's claim that everything was fine. They both felt bad about what had happened. Jackie did not want to be alone, and Henry agreed to go to her place and stay the night with her. Once they arrived at her place, they got into another argument about their relationship, and Henry beat her again.

After that incident, they decided to see a counselor. The remainder of December was spent trying to break off the relationship. It was difficult for both of them. Jackie would decide to end the relationship and then a couple of days later would want to get back with him. The same was true for Henry. They ended the relationship in early January.

Henry and Jackie drank a lot. They claimed that every time an incident occurred, they had been drinking. Drinking did not always lead to an abusive incident, however. In any case, they both admitted that alcohol made the physical violence worse. Henry and Jackie indicated that much of the violence had to do with jealousy and power.

Jackie and Henry were upset about what had culminated in their relationship. Henry felt bad that he had hurt Jackie, and Jackie still loved Henry, even six months after they broke up. Jackie was not sure if she would ever get over Henry, and Henry doubted whether he was mature enough to handle a relationship.

COUPLE 3: FRED AND ANN

Fred was 28 years old and white; he grew up in Kentucky. He had a high school diploma. Two months before we met, he had been fired from his job in a small midwestern city; he had worked for a company that produced elevators. A month after he lost his job, he moved to a neighboring town to live with his brother. He continues to live there to date. He works on his brother's farm to obtain food and shelter while receiving unemployment.

There were 11 children in Fred's family. Seven of the children were from his parents' previous marriages. He was the second child from his parents' marriage. He had an older brother and younger brother and sister. He had neither experienced nor witnessed violence when he was young. In prior relationships, he had never hit a woman.

Ann was 21 years old and white; she was born in Tennessee. Like Fred, Ann had a high school diploma. Just before she married Fred, in the summer of 1984, she had been laid off from her job; she had worked for a television company in a midwestern city. When she had married, she babysat to supplement their income. When she and Fred separated in February 1985, she returned home and spent her time babysitting until she got a full-time job. The following September, she found a full-time job with a company that made greeting cards. In October 1985, she quit her job due to personality conflicts with her employer. The last time we talked, she was looking for a fast-food job until something more stable came up. Currently, she lives in a small midwestern community with a man she had been dating since her divorce. He is related to Fred.

Ann was the youngest of two children. She had an older brother. She said that her parents had been strict with her because she was the only girl. There had been a lot of fighting between her brother and herself. Though she indicated that there had been no physical violence between her parents, she recalled them verbally fighting a lot. Ann had never experienced any violence in a relationship prior to Fred.

Her feelings about her parents were ambiguous. She talked about how her parents financially helped her and Fred get started in their marriage, but she then claimed that they intruded too much in their relationship, that her mother was over too much and would not let Fred and Ann live their own lives. Her parents asked her to move back home when she separated from Fred, and while she claimed their support helped her through the divorce, as time passed, she started having problems at home. She could not go out without checking with them. She had to be home at a specific time. Ann ran away from home twice during my interviews with her. She felt that they had too much control over her life.

Fred and Ann met in the spring of 1981 at a county fair. Ann was 17 and Fred was 25. Fred said that he was attracted to Ann because she was good looking and she liked many of the same things that he liked. He felt that they had a lot of things in common. Ann said that Fred "treated her nice." Fred was never violent to Ann while they were dating or during their engagement.

They were married in the summer of 1984. They bought a house in the country. Ann's parents helped with the downpayment. Her parents also spent money and time helping them fix it up. Fred and Ann both mentioned that while they appreciated her parents' help, it created problems for them. They were always over, instructing them as to what needed to be done around the house and what role each was expected to play in the marriage. Ann and Fred interpreted this as a violation of their privacy and independence.

Fred indicated that there was only one violent incident that occurred between Ann and himself. It happened just before Christmas 1984. He said that one night he had been lying on the floor watching television and Ann came up and stepped on his head. He said he thought that she stepped on him because he was not paying attention to her. He turned over and hit her in the leg, causing a bad bruise. Again, Fred did not recall any incidents aside from this one.

The story is quite different from interviews with Ann. She said that in November 1984, they started having problems in their marriage. Fred would return home from work, eat dinner, and then go out to a bar. As the weeks passed, he came home later and later. When he arrived home, he would want to have sex. When Ann started refusing him because he was drunk, he started to force her into it. Ann now sees that she experienced many instances of marital rape. She noted that he would "beat on her" until she agreed to have intercourse. When that would not work, he would tie her legs and arms to the bed.

It was very difficult for me to understand how the violence evolved over time between Fred and Ann. Because Fred denied all but a December incident, I had to obtain the information from Ann. Ann said that things got worse from December 1984 until the spring of 1985, but she could not specifically recount each incident of violence in the order that they had happened, the cause of the specific incident, or the nature of the violence. Rather, she talked about the general form and nature of the violence and would mention specific incidents of violence only when she could remember them.

It is clear from my interviews with Ann that Fred was quite abusive. It appeared that in December 1984, he began controlling where she would go. One day she wanted to go fishing by herself. Fred removed the battery from her car so that she could not go. Fred started to throw things around, which frightened Ann. One night he came home drunk and wanted to have sex. She refused and went into the living room to watch television. He want into the living room and threw the television on the floor and told her she was not watching television. Fred was sometimes violent toward their pets. Ann loved dogs and owned a few. Fred came to believe that Ann loved the dogs more than him. One night Fred hit one of her dogs on the head with a snow shovel because it was barking outside. Ann was very hurt by the incident.

She recalls many nights of being raped in January and February 1985. The violence also took more life-threatening forms, as when he chased her around with a butcher knife. One day she ran out of the house as he was chasing her with the knife, and she screamed to the neighbors for help. They did not respond; according to Ann, they said they did not want to get involved. One of her dogs was following her, and as she was encouraging the dog to jump over the fence to the neighbor's yard so that Fred could not hurt it, Fred grabbed the dog and knifed it. Just before Ann left Fred in February, there was an incident where he brought a rattlesnake into the house to tease her. Ann was allergic to snakes and became hysterical. The neighbors finally arrived and forced Fred to get rid of it.

Ann separated from Fred in February 1985 and decided she would divorce him. She went back home. When Fred found out that she filed for the divorce, he was furious. One day in March, Fred ran Ann off the road as she was driving to a shopping mall. When Ann realized what was happening, she stopped the car and ran across the road to a plaza where she knew there would be people around. She began to climb a fence to get away from Fred. Fred grabbed her off the fence and, in the course of it, tore her hand. He threw her over the car and told her that she was going home with him to call her lawyer to drop the divorce proceedings. Ann managed to call the police when she got to the house without Fred knowing. When the police came, Fred was furious and took out his gun to use on her. The police arrested him. She returned to him for about a week and a half in April. From May until October, Ann went back to Fred seven different times.

Ann eventually charged Fred with assault and battery, rape, and theft (he once stole her car keys). They divorced in June 1985. Fred was put on probation for a year due to the charges against him.

After the divorce, Ann began seeing Fred's cousin. However, at the same time, she was trying to get back with Fred. When she realized in October that there was nothing left between Fred and her, she decided to see more of Fred's cousin. They moved in together in November. From what Ann told me, Fred was dating but was not seeing anyone seriously.

Ann indicated that violence typically resulted from arguments about money, sex, drugs, and alcohol. Fred would often use the money he was making to go to bars, instead of paying essential bills, such as the mortgage. Ann indicated that she still loved Fred but believed that he was too immature to handle a relationship.

COUPLE 4: MIKE AND KAY

Mike was 29 years old and white; he grew up in Georgia. Mike attended college for two years. In the fall of 1984, he entered a two-year technical school to study computer electronics. To date, he has not returned to school to complete the degree. He has worked in several fast-food establishments and department stores for the past 8 years. Three months prior to our initial interview, he began working two jobs. In our last interview, he indicated that he had been promoted in his department store job and was going to be receiving a full-time position. He planned to quit his other job.

Mike came from a small family and had only one younger brother. His father had died when he was very young; he had been raised by a stepfather, who had died in 1978. Soon after I met with Mike, he discovered that his stepfather was not his real father and began to understand a bit more about their relationship during his childhood. He noted that they had never been close and that his stepfather had always favored his younger brother. Mike had felt unloved and unwanted by him. In addition, Mike had been born with a malfunctioning heart. He had undergone operations in 16 years. He noted that his parents had not been allowed to visit him every day while he was in the hospital; they had been allowed to visit on the day of the operation and then every three or four days afterwards. As a result, Mike had grown up feeling that no one cared about him. In early interviews, Mike frequently talked about feeling depressed. He attributed it to the new information about his stepfather and stored-up resentment regarding the fact that no one had cared for him when he was young.

Mike claimed that he had been punished quite a bit when he was young, but he did not consider himself to have been abused. He had not witnessed violence between his parents. He had never been violent to women in prior relationships.

After his stepfather's death, his mother remarried. Mike was not close to either of them. He recently had been working on getting closer to his mother. He felt better about their relationship as he shared with her his feelings of the past and current problems with his violence.

Kay is 30 years old and white; she is from Alabama. She had a secretarial certificate, and soon after her separation from Mike, she obtained a secretarial job at a large midwestern university. In many ways, it changed her life significantly. It was the first time in many years that she had worked. She felt more confident and in control of her life.

Kay's father had died when she was seven, and her mother had had a nervous breakdown a half-year later. Subsequently, Kay had been placed in a foster home while her mother was taken to an institution. For the next 10 years, she had lived with five different families. She had run away from each home because, as she said, "They couldn't get it through their heads that I had a family." She had held onto memories of the first seven years of her life and had felt that each family she stayed with was no match for the family she once had. When she was not living with a family, she had stayed in temporary homes until a more permanent home became available. Kay never had experienced or witnessed abuse as a child.

Kay described her mother as an adolescent and not someone she could count on while growing up. She said that as a consequence of living in different homes, she became a very submissive person. She would be very cooperative to gain others' approval. She argued that this partially explains why she allowed the domestic violence to happen with Mike. It was always important to her to get along with everybody.

At age 17, she had been released from the courts. Her future looked bleak and frightening. She had not known where she would live or how she would survive, especially because she was then in high school and would not be able to obtain a good job until she graduated. Consequently, she married a man that she had been dating since she was 15. The marriage did not work out; by age 18, she was divorced. Six months later, she married a man she had been dating for two or three months. She had a child when she was 19. She had divorced again at 21. She wanted more children and was looking for a man who was also interested in raising a family. She started dating Mike, who she discovered was also interested in having children. At about age 23, Kay married Mike. Violence had not existed in any of her relationship prior to Mike.

Mike was Kay's second husband's best friend. They used to play cards together. Mike had gone away to college for two years, and when he returned, he found out that Kay had divorced his friend. He started visiting her, taking her places (Kay lost her car to her second husband), and helping her fix up her apartment. He eventually moved in with her. When Kay's apartment manager found out that Mike was staying with her, however, he asked them either to get married or for Mike to leave. They decided to get married; they married in the spring of 1978. Mike was not violent to Kay prior to their marriage, although Kay recalled Mike having a temper while they were dating. When Mike would get angry with friends or co-workers, Kay recalled thinking, "Boy, I'm glad he's not angry with me." Kay never thought that he would be physically violent to her.

Kay indicated that the first incident occurred two months after they married. They went on a picnic with Kay's children and Kay permitted her 2-year-old son to go wading in the lake. He came down with an ear infection and Mike was upset. He told her that she was a poor, unfit mother. He hit her that night, which resulted in a bruise on her face and a cut lip. After he hit her, he threatened divorce and left the house. Kay sat and cried. She felt devastated because she had been married twice already and thought another divorce would make her a three-time loser. When Mike returned, she frantically apologized for upsetting him and pleaded with him to stay. He agreed to work things out with her. However, Kay notes that the violence continued from then on.

Mike cites the first incident as occurring approximately two years into the marriage. He recalls that at the time, Kay was two months pregnant with their first child and he shoved her down on the floor. He does not remember why he did that. The next incident that he remembers occurred in about 1982. He recalls slapping her hard. Mike did not remember what the incident was about, but he did note that most of their arguments were over money. The final incident that he remembers occurred before they separated in March, 1985. He said that she tried to leave the living room and he threw her back into the room. He claims that he did not hit her.

Kay's recollection of Mike's abuse through the years was much more detailed and severe than Mike's accounts. She noted that early in their marriage, she experienced "mental attacks" from Mike. For example, if she took too long at the grocery store, he would yell at her when she came home. She was not to visit her friends, and she was to keep the house spotless. If any of Mike's demands were not met, he would become verbally abusive to her.

Kay described the second violent incident but could not remember when it happened. She remembers that he got her down on the bed, grabbed her throat, and started choking her. She was telling him to stop, and he threatened to kill her if she did not keep quiet. She did not remember what the incident was about. She notes that after that choking incident, he started to push, shove, hit, and throw her around. She says she worked hard at not getting him upset.

Kay did indicate that Mike pushed, slapped, and threw her around during her pregnancy with their first child. She said that was when she started seeking help from local church women. They offered their homes if she needed a place to stay.

The next violent incident that Kay remembers occurred about in 1982. When their first child was about a year-and-a-half, he came down with a nasal infection. Kay called Mike because she needed him to take her and the child to the doctor; Mike refused. Kay then called his mother, and she came to pick them up. On the way home from the doctor's office, Mike caught up with them on the road. He motioned his mother to pull over. He stormed out of the car, and Kay knew he was mad. He came up to the car, forced Kay out, and began yelling at her. He threatened to kill her. He demanded that she immediately come home with him. She refused because she feared what he might do to her when they got home. She screamed for help, and a stranger finally helped Kay get away from Mike. Kay immediately went to a shelter for abused women. After a week, Kay returned to Mike because her church minister had told her that he had changed.

The church minister believed that part of Mike's violence had to do with the fact that they were experiencing a lot of financial stress. As a result, the church took over payment of their bills; this continued for two years. In the meantime, Mike and Kay had another child, and Mike continued working at fast-food establishments. In the fall of 1984, a new minister at their church decided that Mike and Kay would have to assume sole responsibility for their finances.

The next violent incident occurred during Christmas of 1984. The family was at Mike's mother's house helping her put up her Christmas tree. The youngest child was screaming and crying, and Kay decided to put him to bed. That did not stop the child from crying, and Mike went into the bedroom and beat up the child. The next morning, Kay looked at the child, who was covered with bruises, and realized that Mike was now moving his violence onto the children. She immediately took the children to her local church, and they said that she should report the child abuse to the local officials. She complied and then went to the women's shelter. When she called Mike the next day, he frantically apologized and convinced her to return home so that the family could spend Christmas together.

After that incident, they began to go to couple's counseling. One day in mid-February, they were on their way home from a counseling session when Mike became verbally abusive. Kay was frightened. They stopped at a grocery store to get some household items, and Kay took the children to the manager's office to get away from Mike. She was frightened of what he might do when they got home. She and her children went to the shelter. She stayed there for a week and then returned home.

Kay returned home on the condition that she could get a job. However, she soon found that every time she scheduled an interview, Mike refused to let her go. In early March, they had an argument about it. Kay says that Mike just went crazy. He got out his guns and loaded them. He said that he was going to go out and rob a bank since he could not adequately provide for his family. Kay tried to calm him and reminded him that their counselor told them that if they ever got into a fight to go take a walk until things calmed down. Kay said she was going to do that. She went to the door to leave, Mike grabbed her, ran her into the wall, and then threw her on the floor. Their son ran over to a neighbor's house and called Mike's mother. Mike's mother arrived and said that she was going to take the children because their home was too unsettled. Mike and Kay admitted that there were some problems between them.

To resolve the situation, Mike agreed to enter the psychiatric ward at a nearby hospital. Mike was there for several days. When Kay found out he was coming home, she packed her bags and took the children over to the home of her brother and sister-in-law. Kay said that when they did not want her anymore, she went to the women's shelter. She finally rented an apartment, where she had been living from our initial interview until our last interview. After Kay left Mike in early March, 1985, Mike traveled south for a couple of months. Upon his return, he got his own place, put their house up for sale, and entered the male batterer's group. He entered individual counseling as well. Kay found a job and also entered individual counseling.

Kay and Mike remained separated for the length of time I interviewed them. In early September, they entered marital counseling. Throughout the 4-month period, Mike and Kay worked on solving the problems in their marriage, including Mike's violent behavior. Mike was not abusive to Kay during the period of time that I met with him. In time, they began to communicate more and understand each other better. I briefly talked to Kay in November, and she indicated that Mike would be moving into the apartment with her and the children just before Christmas. They appeared to have resolved many of their problems.

Mike and Kay agreed that the violence in their relationship stemmed from Mike wanting to control Kay's life. He wanted to have the power to tell her what to do, where to go, and who to see. Mike said that he would not allow Kay to be herself and Kay noted that the minute she challenged his authority, he would get mad and often become violent. Kay said that the reason she put up with the violence for so many years was because she thought that was what she had to do in order to have the additional children that she wanted. She noted that it was her understanding that the violence came with the territory. It was not until she felt that she could not put up with the violence any longer that she was finally motivated to leave Mike.

COUPLE 5: LARRY AND TERRI

Larry was aged 27 years and white; he was raised in New Jersey. He attended the University of Iowa for two years. After dropping out of school, he want to work full time. Currently, he works as a research assistant at a large university in the Midwest. He planned to leave that job by the end of 1985 to work full time at starting his own advertising business.

Larry grew up in a Catholic family of five children, with an older brother, a younger sister, and two younger brothers. Larry had done all the "trail blazing" in the family. He drank and used drugs heavily during adolescence and early adulthood. He had recovered from his drug addiction and had not taken a drink for three years.

Larry claimed to have been spanked and slapped a lot when he was young but does not remember any uncontrolled incidents. He remembered his parents had argued a lot, often after he and his father had had a confrontation. He does not remember physical violence ever occurring between his parents. He had heard from his sister that some violence occurred after Larry moved out.

In my initial interview with him, he had recently found out from his father that his mother was an alcoholic, and when she had gotten drunk, she would get physically violent with Larry's father. Larry's father had recently separated from her, was planning to divorce, and had become involved with another woman. The news of his mother's problems was difficult for Larry to deal with, but he had come to accept it by our last interview.

Larry remembered coming from a home environment where there had been very little physical affection and sharing of feelings. He indicated that part of his current problem in dealing with anger was not only because he had never been given the opportunity to express such a feeling when he was young, but also because he had never been taught how to appropriately express it. Larry had never been violent to women in prior relationships to Terri.

Terri was 25 years old and white; she was born in Louisiana and later her parents moved to New York. Like Larry, she attended college at the University of Iowa. After graduation, she accepted a one-year position at a large midwestern company. The following year, she moved to a small midwestern city and worked as a part-time research assistant. In August 1985, she found a full-time job working for displaced homemakers.

Terri grew up in a Catholic family of seven children. She had been closest to her younger brother and sister; her older brother committed suicide at the age of 19; Terri was 14 years old at the time. In our interviews, she indicated that she was beginning to work out in individual therapy her feelings regarding her brother's death.

There had been no physical violence in Terri's family, but she does remember her father being loud and angry for many years. Terri had frequently used drugs during adolescence. She had stopped early in college because she feared flunking out of school and because a man that she was dating did not approve of it. She does not recall ever experiencing violence in prior relationships.

Larry and Terri met in a college class in the fall of 1981. They kept in contact through a mutual friend and eventually became close friends, but never seriously dated. Instead, they and four other people would often go out together as a group. When Terri left her temporary job and moved to a midwestern city, she met up with Larry again. She obtained a part-time job in a lab where he was a research assistant. They started dating in the spring of 1983. They moved in together in the summer of 1984.

Both Larry and Terri recall Larry being violent as early as September of 1983. They mention this period as a time when Larry was intensely angry and always in a rage, but neither one of them could determine the source of his anger. They would discuss it, and although Larry was aware of what was going on, he could not explain why it was occurring. He would typically throw small objects, such as a telephone book or brush.

Terri had been living with Larry for a couple of weeks in September until her new apartment became available. The living arrangement may have put a strain on their relationship. Terri remembers that at that time she talked to a friend, expressing her concern that he might eventually be physically violent to her.

After September, Larry was not violent until November, when Terri moved in with him. Again, Larry would be feeling extremely angry and would throw things, kick something, or slam things around. Terri said that part of his anger may have come from such matters as the logistics of how they were going to live together, such as the division of labor. Larry also mentioned the new living arrangement as putting a strain on their relationship, and he indicated that working together in the same lab was getting to be too difficult. He said they were beginning to expect more out of each other at work than they would expect out of other co-workers. In addition, in the middle of November, each of them stopped smoking. The arguments and acts of violence continued until early January 1985.

Larry provided a detailed description of what happened between November 1984 and January 1985. About two weeks after they quit smoking, they were having an argument and he threw a bottle of hand lotion down the hall. Terri was not in the hall, but Larry noted that the act was directed at her. Three weeks later, they were having another argument at their coffee table, and he got angry and flipped the coffee table over. Four or five weeks after that, they were arguing again, and he threw a television remote controller at her. Larry indicated that Terri would often go to bed and refuse to talk about problems that he wanted to settle. When she would leave, he would follow her into the bedroom and behave violently to let her know that he was angry. One time he put a hole in the bedroom wall; another time he slammed the bedroom door so hard that he tore the trim off the door; and still another time, he smashed a bedroom chair. He even went so far as attempting to double over the bedroom mattress while Terri was on it.

In the early spring of 1985, another argument arose, and Larry grabbed Terri's shoulders and shook her; he told her that he needed to leave or else he was going to smash her. He came back after he had calmed down. A month or two later, they were having an argument outside, and Larry grabbed Terri, pushed her up against their car, and yelled in her face. That was the last incident to occur before I met with each of them.

Larry and Terri started individual counseling in early 1985, mainly because they felt that they each had to work out individual issues that were troubling themselves. In my initial interview with each of them, both Larry and Terri mentioned that they were not sure if the problem was one of Larry needing to control his violence or if it had to do with some deeper issue, namely how they communicated with each other. Larry decided not to enter the male batterer's group and instead stayed with his individual counseling to see if he could work out their problems through that method of treatment.

In early July 1985, Larry and Terri entered couple's counseling. At that time, they began to explore the source of their problems. In mid-July, they separated. Just before the separation, another violent incident occurred. Again, they had been arguing. Larry wanted to leave and calm down before the argument escalated. He asked Terri for his keys. She would not give them to him. She started to walk away, he grabbed them from her, they fell on the floor and as he bent down to get them, she started pounding her fists on his back. He responded by turning over and pushing her several times, but not hard enough to cause her to fall to the floor.

They eventually moved back in together in mid-September. Though the violence stopped, the arguments did not. They agreed to continue couple's counseling until they were able to get things settled between themselves. It was unclear how long that would take. They did mention that the counseling was helping them tremendously. They were learning about each other and what some of the sources of their arguments were.

From their accounts over time, it is clear that the majority of their problems, whether verbal or physical in nature, were due to miscommunication and misinterpretation of each other. For example, when Larry would give his opinion on how the thermostat in the house was to be operated and Terri disagreed with that opinion, Larry would interpret her disagreement as implying that his opinion was worthless. Terri's intent, however, was not to downgrade Larry's opinion but rather to suggest an alternative way of doing things. Larry would get angry because his opinion was being challenged, Terri would respond to the anger with anger of her own, and the discussion would escalate into a full-blown argument. In couple's counseling, they were not only beginning to understand that this was occurring, but were also learning how arguments and violence might be avoided.

COUPLE 6: DOUG AND WENDY

Doug was 34 years old and white; he was born in Texas. He went to college for two years. His employment status has been unstable for many years. He has had a few jobs but largely has been unemployed for most of his adult life. Currently, he is unemployed. Doug had been a drug addict and alcoholic in his early adult life. He has not engaged in any form of substance abuse for the last three years.

Doug came from a Catholic family. He was the oldest of seven children. He described the relationship between his parents as poor. He felt that he did not have good parents. He said they were not very loving and caring. Doug claimed that he had been hit a lot by his mother while growing up. There had not been much physical violence between his parents.

In prior relationships, Doug had been repeatedly abusive to women. He claimed that this was largely because soon after high school, he had been put in jail for breaking and entering and had some bad experiences with inmates and guards who physically and psychologically abused him.

Doug married at the age of 24. He indicated that he had been very violent to his wife, often raping her. They had three children. They had been married for eight years but were separated the last four years of their marriage.

Doug told me many stories of being abusive to women he dated after his relationship to his wife. He recounted only one specific story of where he was physically violent with another man. Though he claims that he sometimes found himself in a fight with another man, he did not view fighting with other males as a pattern to his behavior. He claims that he never saw himself looking for a fight with another man, but he often found himself wanting to fight in his relationships with women.

Wendy was 26 years old and white; she was originally from Idaho. Wendy had attended college for two years. When I first met her, she had been on maternity leave from her job as a secretary for an insurance company in a small midwestern city. She was still working part-time, however, because she was the the company's only secretary and her boss needed her help. Several months later, she was fired from her job and began receiving unemployment benefits. The last time we talked, she was looking for a job but was not optimistic that she could find a position that was comparable in salary to what she had previously earned. She was quite satisfied with her unemployment status because she could adequately live on the monthly checks she was receiving, was able to spend time with her newborn child, and was able to become more involved at the halfway house where she enjoyed volunteering.

Wendy had a sister who was 19 years older than she, from her mother's first marriage; she also had a younger brother. She was very close to her younger brother but did not remember much interaction with her older stepsister. Wendy says her parents had been strong disciplinarians, but she remembers only one incident where she thinks she had probably been abused. She had been 15 years old at the time and had run away; she was gone for 48 hours. When she returned, her mother and brother held her down while her dad beat her. She said that incident broke her spirit. After that, she claimed she grew to seek their approval. When she turned to drugs and alcohol as an adolescent, she had hidden it from them. She had smoked cigarettes for 12 years and she indicated that her parents still do not know. To date, she does not share her private life with them. Wendy had never seen her dad hit her mom.

At the age of 18, Wendy became engaged. The engagement lasted for six years, and then broke up. A man she was living with prior to Doug became physically violent to her one day. She subsequently left him and was never involved with him again.

Doug and Wendy met at a bar one night in February 1984. They got along well, and Doug followed her home. He spent the night, and they lived together from then on. They lived at Wendy's apartment until September 1984, at which time her apartment manager found out that Doug was living with her and evicted her. They subsequently moved to

Doug's place. Wendy also found out she was pregnant with Doug's child.

Wendy was attending individual counseling at the time, and her counselor had encouraged her to write a contract with Doug that would protect her if Doug ever wanted to remove her from his place. She agreed, and the contract included paying Doug's rent, utilities, and food in exchange for living there. Wendy notes that when she moved into Doug's place and then discovered she was pregnant, their relationship began to sour. She said that the contract and pregnancy were the cause. She felt that by writing the contract, she was implying to Doug that she did not trust him when she really did. She merely wanted to protect herself. Moreover, she said that the contract gave Doug an excuse for never being committed to Wendy because he could always come back and say, "No, I'm just your landlord." In fact, that is how Doug described to me the nature of his relationship with Wendy. He never admitted that it was anything other than a landlord–renter relationship.

The pregnancy was an additional problem. Doug was not happy about it, and never really indicated to Wendy that he wanted the child and was willing to take responsibility for raising it. Moreover, Wendy's parents had trouble accepting the fact that she was going to have an illegitimate child, which created a heartache for Wendy. This naturally affected her interaction with Doug.

Wendy noted that Doug started dating other women after she told him about her pregnancy. He would not come home or would come home late at night. The physical violence began in February 1985. Up until that point, Doug had not been abusive toward Wendy.

The first incident occurred one Saturday night when Wendy came home late. When she drove up to the apartment, she saw a stranger's car parked outside. The lights were off in Doug's place, and soft music was playing. As she was locked out, she started banging on the door to be let in. When Doug answered and she came in, Wendy found another woman there. Doug said that the woman's husband had been threatening to hurt her, and she wanted to know if she could spend the night. Wendy agreed and said she could sleep on the couch. She then went to do some laundry.

When she returned, she decided to go into the bedroom and read. She got up to go to the kitchen, get some juice, and take her vitamins. As she passed Doug and the woman in the living room, she saw them lying on the couch, partially undressed, and kissing. Wendy got angry. She called Doug into the kitchen. He went into the kitchen and told Wendy that he thought it would be best if she left. She started yelling at him. He responded by grabbing her and attempting to throw her out the front door. She got away and ran back into the kitchen. He came back after her, grabbed her by the back of the head, and pulled her to the front door again. She lost a handful of hair. She ran back into the kitchen because she was not fully dressed, and she knew she could not leave just yet. The third time he grabbed her, she fell, and he dragged her once more across the floor to the front door. He then stopped. Wendy got dressed and immediately left. She had decided she would leave him. The following day, Doug called her, apologized, and asked her to come back. She agreed.

The following Monday night, Doug had not returned by 1:00 A.M. Wendy suspected Doug was with a woman, and when she called her place, she found out that he was there. She immediately packed enough clothes for the rest of the week and went to stay at a girlfriend's house. Tuesday afternoon, Wendy went to the grocery store on her lunch break. Doug saw her at the store. He wanted to talk to her, but she refused. As they left the grocery store, Doug got in front of Wendy and grabbed her glasses off her face and smashed them; Wendy was upset because she is legally blind without her glasses. She walked to her car, and when she got there, Doug started apologizing frantically. They went to a counselor on Tuesday night. The counselor advised them to separate for awhile until they got some help. However, Wendy returned to Doug that night.

The next incident occurred in mid-March. Wendy had found out that Doug had spent another night with a woman. The night that she found out, they were in the bedroom and Wendy told him that she was leaving him. He had been lying on the bed, and he rolled over and sat on her legs and started hitting her in the face. Wendy was able to get out from under him, but then he got up, grabbed her, and threw her up against the wall. At that point, Wendy was afraid to leave because she was afraid of what he might do as a result. She decided to stay.

The next incident occurred in April. Wendy and Doug went out with some friends one night. Presumably, Wendy had said something that Doug interpreted as an insult to him. He got angry and left. Doug did not come home that night. The following night, Wendy had some friends over. Doug came home late and went into the bedroom. Wendy followed him to see why he was upset. They started to talk about the previous night, and the conversation escalated into an argument. Doug hit Wendy once on the temple and once in the eye. She screamed, and one of her friends came in to help.

In early interviews with Wendy, she still loved Doug and wanted to work things out with him. She was hoping that his participation in the male batterer's group would help. Later on, she came to believe that Doug wanted complete control of her and that any time she did something that he did not want, he would be violent.

A month after I initially talked to Doug and Wendy, two more violent incidents occurred. They got into an argument one night regarding the fact that Wendy would not agree to sell some of her diamonds so that they could go to a convention. The argument escalated, and Wendy decided that she would take the newborn and spend the night at her girlfriend's house. On her way out, he grabbed her by the arm, threw her on the couch and pinned her down. He then ripped her glasses off. The incident stopped, but Wendy was afraid to leave, so she stayed and slept on the sofa that night and for the following two weeks.

The second incident was more severe. Wendy had agreed to go to an AA meeting with Doug one night. She had interpreted his suggestion as asking her for a date, whereas Doug saw it more as a meeting that might help her out. When they arrived at the meeting place, Doug said that he would watch the child in the car while she went in. Wendy did not want to go to the meeting by herself; they began arguing. Doug demanded that she go to the meeting and Wendy refused. Doug finally got out of the car, went around to her side, grabbed her by the back of the head, pulled her out of the car, and started smacking her. He ripped her glasses off. He threatened to break her nose and smash her head into a nearby wall. She then agreed to go to the meeting but said she was going to take the baby. He refused to give her the baby. He told her to go to the meeting and that if she called the police when she got there, he was going to kill the baby. Neighbors heard the arguing and called the police. The police came but left after Wendy and Doug reassured them that everything was fine.

The last incident occurred in early September. They got into an argument one morning regarding the fact that Wendy had asked Doug frequently during the previous week to buy an item for the apartment, and Doug still had not done it. Wendy got angry and started yelling at Doug. She grabbed one of the pillows off the bed and threw it at him, but it missed him. He got up, grabbed her arms and put them behind her back, pushed her down the hall into the baby's room, and started hitting her in the face. His blows resulted in Wendy having two blacks eyes and a bruised face. He then dragged her into the living room and hit her in the face again. This time, he cut open her forehead and eyelid. He then stopped.

No further incidents occurred because Wendy left Doug several days later. She eventually charged him with assault and battery, and he was sentenced to a year in prison. The last time I talked with Wendy, Doug was undergoing psychiatric evaluation.

Wendy felt that although she did the best thing by leaving him and bringing charges against him, she still loved him. On Doug's part, he believed that his violence was due to the fact that Wendy provoked him. He felt that if there was anything he learned from his experience with Wendy, it was that another person could provoke him into violence.

COUPLE 7: KEVIN AND LISA

Kevin was 34 years old and white; he was born in North Dakota. Kevin had attended college for a year or two and then was drafted. He had returned to college in 1974 on a military scholarship and had completed an engineering degree. After graduation, he had re-entered the military until about age 32. At that time, he had fulfilled all of his duties with the military and wanted to try civilian life. He applied for a job at a government corporation in the Midwest and received the position.

Kevin and Lisa had been suffering financial problems since he left the military. He had taken a $10,000 pay cut from what he was previously earning, and he and Lisa could not manage to make ends meet, especially because they had become grossly in debt just before he left the military. Their current plans were for Kevin to accept a high-paying position overseas in January 1986 and for the family to move there. The move would enable them to eventually climb out of debt. They would live there for about four years and return to the United States when their oldest son reached high school age.

Kevin was raised in a southern Baptist environment. He had one older sister and two younger sisters. He claimed that his father had been a very physical person. Every time he and his older sister had a disagreement, his father would force them to physically fight it out. To this day, Kevin does not get along with his older sister. His relationship with his younger sisters, he described as excellent. In fact, he said they ended up idolizing him.

Both his father and mother had been very physical disciplinarians. Kevin recounted several stories of beatings. Despite the physical abuse Kevin received, he had never witnessed violence between his parents. His parents had divorced when he was 11 years old. His siblings had stayed with his mother, they had moved to a larger city, and his mother had obtained a job. She remarried, but 30 days after they married, Kevin's stepfather stole his mother's savings and left town. Kevin's mother had the marriage annulled and never spoke to the man again. Kevin's father had also remarried; his second wife died in 1984, and he remarried again in June 1985. Kevin described his relationship with his father as poor. Although his father had never drunk at home when Kevin was young, Kevin thought he had been an alcoholic. He often remembered smelling liquor on him. He did not see his dad between the ages of 12 and 18. To this day, he never shares much with his father. In prior relationships, Kevin had never hit another woman.

Lisa was 34 years old and white; she was also born in North Dakota. Lisa had a college degree in education. She did not work while married to Kevin, because they had both agreed that she would remain at home with their children until they were older.

Lisa's parents had been divorced when she was 11. Her mother had remarried shortly thereafter, and though it was again an unsuccessful marriage, she stayed in it for several years. Her father had remarried within a year of the divorce and currently remains in that marriage. Lisa was the oldest child and had a younger brother. She also had a half-brother from her mother's remarriage and a half-brother from her father's remarriage.

Lisa remembered domestic violence at home while growing up. Additionally, she recalled that her mother frequently had physically abused her. She indicated that the divorce between her parents had been very nasty; there had been many court proceedings over money. After the divorce, Lisa's stepmother often called her to find out how their money was being spent and to hear the latest escapade of Lisa's stepfather. Lisa felt caught in the middle. As a result, she does not want to repeat divorce in her own life because she does not want her children to go through what she did.

Her relationship with her younger brother was not very close. At a hearing to resolve a custody dispute over her brother, she had testifed for her father, claiming that the man her mother married was a womanizer, an alcoholic, and physically abusive. Lisa believed it was not a good environment for her brother to grow up in; aside from that, she felt he needed a better male figure as a role model.

The relationship between Lisa and her parents has gone through several cycles. While Kevin and Lisa were overseas, there was little communication with them. When Kevin and Lisa returned to the states, she talked to them more often. She described her communication with her mother as always being fairly close. She was also beginning to get closer to her father. She had never been close to him while growing up.

In prior relationships, Lisa remembered that a man she was dating had pushed her and another man whom she was rather serious with was violent on two occasions. However, she did not see herself as having gone from one violent relationship to the next.

Kevin and Lisa met during their first year in college through a mutual friend. They dated on and off for about 18 months. Then Kevin got drafted, did a year of basic training, and they married when he got his first duty station. They moved about 22 times while Kevin was in the military. They have been married for about 14 years and have three sons.

Kevin recalled being somewhat physically violent to Lisa when they were dating. Lisa did not think that happened. Kevin said he would typically shake her and mentioned that it occurred (and continued to occur) in instances where he had made up his mind that things were going to be a certain way.

Lisa remembered the first incident of violence as occurring about a year after their marriage. Kevin hit her in the midst of an argument, but she did not recall what the argument was about. The next time she remembered violence occurring was about four years later when Kevin went back to complete his college degree. Lisa noted that Kevin's violence always seemed to be related to financial stress. Because he was attending school full time, they had some financial difficulties. They were having so many problems in their marriage at that time that they decided to enter marital counseling. They attended the counseling for a month. They never addressed the violence, but rather the fact that the nature of their relationship was more indicative of a mother–father than wife–husband relationship. The counseling did not seem to help deter the abuse, because the violence continued from that point on. After he completed his degree, they moved to where Kevin could attend flight school for two years. Lisa said the violence again occurred and was more severe.

It was difficult to learn about specific violent incidents from Lisa. She primarily spoke about the general nature of the abuse over the years. She mentioned that as their financial pressures accumulated, the abuse intensified. Kevin gave his account of the abuse over time and noted that it did get more severe, but not because the financial pressures increased. Rather, he said that it was primarily due to whether or not the form of violence he was using was an effective means to control Lisa. He said that Lisa would grow used to each specific form of violence such that, over time, it no longer became an effective means to get what he wanted. Therefore, he needed to use the next degree of violence in order to instill a renewed fear in Lisa, in order to gain what he wanted. So, while early on shaking was enough to frighten her so that she would back down and not challenge his authority, over time the shaking became ineffective so that he had to use pushing. After pushing became ineffective, he progressed to slapping and then to more severe forms of abuse.

Lisa mentioned that it was her belief that there was a high incidence of spouse abuse in the military. She had seen much of it go on. She said that it was probably due to all the stress that the men were under and the long periods of separation from their families. Lisa said that she primarily stayed and took the violence because Kevin was always sorry after an incident had happened. Additionally, because both she and Kevin had come from divorced families, she was determined that they would not end up divorced as well.

When violence occurred early on in their marriage, Lisa remembers withdrawing from Kevin. Within the past six months, however, she had started to strike back. She said she did that because she was tired of being hurt and nothing else seemed to deter the violence. Interestingly enough, this did prove somewhat effective. Kevin was not as violent because he knew he would get hit back and that it would hurt. Kevin himself expressed this feeling to me.

Both Kevin and Lisa admitted that Kevin always wanted to control Lisa's behavior. Lisa said that he was always trying to get her to stop doing whatever she was doing at the time. But Lisa was a fighter and she constantly challenged Kevin's position. Kevin believed that the only way he could overpower her was through physical violence.

In early June 1985, Kevin moved out of the house. He had been physically violent towards their second son. He realized that because he was moving his violence onto his children, he had to leave. He felt that the home was no longer safe, not only for Lisa but also for their children. In late June, they started marital counseling. They discontinued the sessions in late July because they felt they no longer needed it. In early July, Kevin returned home. There were two incidents in July when Kevin was somewhat physically abusive. One was cited by Kevin and the other by Lisa.

One night they were having an argument (Kevin did not remember what the argument was about) and Lisa did not want to argue any more so she decided to leave the room. As she was leaving, Kevin grabbed her by the arm and pulled her back. Lisa ended up with a bruise on her arm. Kevin claimed that his behavior was not intended as an act of violence. They talked about it afterwards, and Kevin convinced her that his intent was not to hurt her.

The other incident happened on a Sunday before I met with Lisa. That Sunday morning, while they were arguing, Kevin threw a coffee cup at her. Lisa claims that, although the act was not that violent, it brought out the fear in family members that the violence was going to start again.

Those incidents were the last ones that were cited by either Kevin or Lisa for the remainder of our interviews. It appeared that over time, Kevin came to accept his violent behavior and was learning how to avoid it. Lisa repeatedly noted in later interviews how Kevin had changed and how their relationship was much better. He had become a mature, responsible person, they communicated with each other more, and when they had disagreements, it did not escalate into violence.

COUPLE 8: BILL AND JANE

Bill was 32 years old and black; he was born in Michigan. He had a high school degree. In 1983, Bill had completed a three-year sentence on a penal farm for beating up his former girlfriend and the man she had been dating. Prior to the penal farm, he had served two years at a state penitentiary for the same charge. He had been on probation for three years after leaving the farm. He then entered a drug addiction program. In 1984, he had obtained a part-time job in a midwestern city through his probation officer; he had lived at a halfway house. He moved into a house with some friends in August 1985 and began taking college classes in the fall at a major university in the Midwest.

The last time I interviewed him, he had been arrested for driving while intoxicated. He said he was on his way to his girlfriend's house to kill her but was picked up by the police for drunk driving. He did not know what he would do with his future. It was unclear whether he would finish his fall classes, and he was thinking of entering the military reserve.

Bill had been raised by his aunt and uncle and thought this was because his mother had wanted to placed him in the care of people who could give him the love and attention she could not. Bill had not gotten along with his mother or father and never communicated with them much. He had been very close to his aunt and uncle. His uncle died of tuberculosis when Bill was nine; his aunt died of cancer six years later. Bill then returned to his mother's home. He had wanted to move in with the woman who used to babysit for him when he lived with his aunt and uncle, but his mother had refused. Bill indicated that as a response to his mother's refusal, he started breaking the law; for example, he had been charged with robbery. He eventually was sent to a detention center. Soon afterwards, his mother sent him to visit the woman Bill wanted to live with. The visit had lasted only a week, and Bill had anticipated a summer stay with her. His mother came for him and he had returned home. Bill noted that again, as a response, he returned to his criminal behavior and was in and out of jails.

Bill has been very abusive to women in prior relationships. He was very violent to the first woman he dated. For a period of time he was a john for prostitutes; one prostitute he fell in love with he also abused. His violent behavior extended to many fights with men.

Because Jane did not participate in this research, the history of this relationship comes from my interviews with Bill. Bill had moved into a halfway house in December 1984. Jane had also been living there. A month later, Bill and Jane started dating. They fell in love. However, early in the relationship, Bill did not trust Jane because he would often see her with other men. Though Bill would get upset, he would continue to put time and effort into their relationship. They would often get into arguments because Bill felt that she was taking advantage of him.

Jane moved out of the halfway house in August. She had several children who were wards of the court, and the only way that she could get them back was to get a job and find her own place. Bill helped her move. At about the same time, Jane became pregnant with Bill's child. In mid-August, Bill moved in with Jane but left a week later because they were not getting along.

The only incident that Bill recounted of being physically violent to Jane occurred the day before he moved Jane to her new place in August. He had called her from work and asked her to drop off a sandwich to him for lunch. Bill was busy at work and had to end the conversation abruptly. Jane thought Bill had hung up on her and was upset. When she dropped off the sandwich, Bill could tell that she was upset and tried to explain to her that he was busy at work and did not mean to cut the conversation short. Jane did not want to listen to his explanation and walked to her car. Bill was angry. As she was driving away, Bill took the plate that the sandwich was on and threw it at her car. He missed the car, and the plate smashed onto a nearby sidewalk.

Bill and Jane continued to have problems in their relationship during the months that Bill and I met. Jane started seeing her ex-boyfriend again, and Bill was jealous. They began to see each other less. Though Bill was still deeply in love with Jane, it appeared that Jane no longer loved Bill.

In my last interview with Bill, his feelings for Jane had taken a turn for the worse. The week before we met, Bill had seen Jane with her ex-boyfriend several times. Bill started drinking again; he had not been drinking for a year. The night before we met, Bill had become drunk and drove over to Jane's house to kill her. He felt that he had taken enough from her. On his way over there, he was picked up by the police for driving while intoxicated. He was arrested and spent the night in jail.

In our last interview, it was unclear how Bill would deal with Jane in the future. He indicated that he still loved her, but because she started seeing her ex-boyfriend again, it made him crazy enough to want to kill her. He did not feel he could control his temper any more and that he had to act on what he felt.

COUPLE 9: FRANK AND NANCY

Frank was 31 years old and black; he grew up in New York. Frank was a graduate of New York University with a degree in public administration. After college, he had worked for a parks and recreation center but left after four years because he had been unhappy with it; he wanted to work with people. He had gone to graduate school in social work, but did not finish. He turned to counseling children at a boys' town for two years. He then worked at a facility for the handicapped for a year and a half. After feeling that he could not do enough for the disadvantaged, he had left the helping profession and obtained his current job, working full time in a factory in the Midwest; he was looking for another job. Prospects include returning to some kind of counseling work.

There were nine siblings in his family. He had three older brothers and sisters, and a younger brother and sister. Frank's father, from his mother's third marriage, had died when Frank was two. Frank was the seventh child from the marriage. The only father that Frank remembered was his mother's fourth husband. They had had two children. They had divorced when Frank was about 15. Frank recalled domestic violence in that marriage.

Frank had not been home much as a child because he had entered a dance group at the age of seven and was continually on the road for nine months out of the year until age 18. Though he had maintained a close relationship with his mother, he had never become close to his siblings as he had seldom been home. He said that they had always looked up to him, however, because he had been the only one of them who made something of his life.

When Frank graduated from college, he had married a woman he had been dating for about a year. They were married for five years and then divorced. They had had two children. Two years after the divorce, they had remarried for another nine months and then had divorced again.

Frank claims that he had not been abusive to women in prior relationships. He said that he had hit two former girlfriends once, but that was because he had been defending himself.

Nancy was 27 years old and white. She was born in Texas. Nancy had a high school degree. After high school, she had worked at a fast food establishment for about a year. She did not work again for about five years and then had worked as a waitress for a couple of years. Currently, she babysits but is looking for another job.

Nancy had an older sister, a younger sister who was handicapped, and a younger brother. While growing up, Nancy had spent much of her time at home caring for her younger sister and brother because both her parents worked. She does not remember violence between her parents. Her father died in 1983 of cancer.

She left home at age 15. At 16, she had married a high school boyfriend. They had one child. They were divorced when she was 19. She indicated that her husband had often taken drugs and could not hold down a job. She remembered that he had hit her a couple of times.

After the divorce, she had run into her junior high sweetheart. They moved in together; she had stayed with him for eight years. They had had two children. She also recalled several incidents of abuse in that relationship.

Frank and Nancy met at a bar one night in July 1984. They had dinner several nights later and started dating. About the same time, Frank started dating someone else. When Nancy found this out from a friend, she was upset and decided to break things off with Frank. Frank then met with Nancy and admitted that he was seeing someone else who was now pregnant with his child and that he was going to marry her. Nancy accepted it and started dating other men.

In early August, Frank came to Nancy and told her that he decided not to marry after all and that he wanted her back. Nancy agreed to start seeing him again. One Sunday morning soon after they got back together, a man who had been dating Nancy stopped by to see her. He wanted to discuss whether or not they would continue dating. Frank did not want Nancy to see or talk to this man. Nancy told Frank that she had to have the opportunity to break things off. She then left the house for a few hours to sever the previous relationship. When she returned, Frank was upset. As she was entering the house, he smacked her on the head and then ran after the man Nancy had been with and told him never to come around again. When he came back into the house, he took Nancy into the bedroom and beat her. Nancy had to go to the hospital. The following day, she received twelve dozen roses (worth $236) from Frank.

Nancy's roommate came to dislike Frank and, in September, moved out. As Nancy could not afford to live in the apartment by herself, she agreed to move in with Frank. In December, Frank was again violent. Nancy's children were being mischievous one afternoon, and Frank reacted by smacking two of the boys so hard that they both had welts on their body. That night, Nancy while attempting to comfort her boys, Frank got angry, told her she was not to baby her children after he had punished them, and then beat her up. That night, Frank cried for two hours and told her that he would never hit her again. Nancy believed him.

Nancy indicated that there was a pattern to Frank's violence. She noted that things would build up, he would be violent, and then he would be apologetic. Every three weeks another incident would occur. Both Nancy and Frank mentioned that they could not trust the other. Frank often indicated that Nancy would lie to him regarding money matters and dating other men. He said that she would not be honest about what she was spending money on, or the fact that she was seeing another man. Nancy said the same things about Frank. While Frank indicated that part of the violence was due to the fact that he was taking responsibility for Nancy's life, Nancy said that Frank wanted to control her life. Through my conversations with both of them, it became clear that Frank was most pleased when Nancy no longer had any friends and she stayed at home.

The next incident occurred in early spring. Nancy went out to a bar one night when Frank had told her not to. When she came home, he started hitting her, and Nancy's daughter called the police. The police came and tried to convince her to prosecute Frank, but she refused because she believed he was trully sorry for what he had done.

The next incident happened in June. Frank had asked Nancy to marry him, and Nancy told him that if he took her out to eat and asked her in the proper fashion, then maybe she could give him an answer. It had appeared that this was what they were going to do, but then Frank could not get a babysitter, and Nancy therefore assumed that they would not go out. That night, Nancy cooked dinner for her children and started playing with them. Frank was upset because he thought they were going to go out. When Nancy told him that they could not do that, Frank reacted by beating her up. Nancy left after the incident and spent the night with a girlfriend. The following day, Frank caught up with Nancy at a parking lot, grabbed her, and attempted to drag her back to his car to take her home. A friend of Nancy's caught up with them and drove Frank away. She stayed at her friends' house, who eventually convinced her to return home and try things with Frank again; she did.

A week later, another incident occurred. Frank had bought Nancy a suit for Christmas, but she did not like it, so he returned it. Frank found out about it and was upset. He took her to the department store to find out from the salesclerk if she had returned the suit. Nancy had called the salesclerk before they got to the store and asked her to lie for her or Frank would beat her up. When they got to the store, the salesclerk covered for her. As they were leaving the store parking lot, the police showed up. Nancy signalled for the policemen to help her get away from Frank because she feared that he might hurt her when they got home. The police escorted her home, and she went to the women's shelter for a couple of days. Nancy returned on the condition that Frank would enter the male batterer's group.

Two incidents occurred in July; in both situations, Nancy and Frank had been arguing. Once he attempted to choke her, and the other time he slapped her across the face. In early August, Nancy left Frank. Frank had said something nasty about Nancy to his friend in front of her. She got upset and told Frank that if he wanted to say something to her, not to say it to his friend in front of her. Frank got mad and told her to go into the bedroom. Nancy knew that he was going to beat her up. At that point, she decided to take her children and leave. She stayed at a friend's house for a week. Frank came over and convinced her to come back. For the remainder of August, all of September and part of October, Frank and Nancy got along well. There were no arguments or physical violence.

The last time I met with Nancy, in mid-October, another violent incident had occurred. They had had an argument regarding whether or not they were going to go out one night. Nancy had assumed that they were going to go out and started getting dressed. Frank got angry that she was planning to go out, and grabbed her and started hitting her. For the first time, Nancy fought back. The police came and Nancy went to her ex-husband's house for the night. Nancy returned to Frank the following day because she had no other place to go. Nancy felt that she would stay until after she got a job and saved some money to move. She projected moving in February 1986.

4
Emotions as Out of Control and Behavior as In and Out of Control

As mentioned in Chapter 1, symbolic interactionists view individuals' interpretations of themselves and others as important in understanding why they behave as they do. In this study, when respondents interpreted themselves or the other, their own or the other's *feelings* and *behavior* were called up and addressed. The batterers made sense of their violence by describing their emotions as out of control and their behavior as in *and* out of control. The victims did not describe their feelings or behavior as in or out of control. When the men described their partner's emotions and behavior, control was not mentioned. When the women discussed their partner's emotions, they did not describe their feelings in terms of control, but they did describe their partner's behavior as in *and* out of control. Therefore, the men only referred to control when describing their own emotions and behavior with respect to violence, and the women only mentioned control when describing the men's behavior. Before presenting evidence that violence is understood in terms of the batterers emotions and behavior being in or out of control, let me make some preliminary remarks.

Among symbolic interactionists, understanding the self has been typically lodged in cognitive terms. As Stryker (1980, p. 153) points out:

The self of the symbolic interactionist has largely been conceptualized in *cognitive* rather than *affective* terms; and the framework's concern with significant symbols, meaning, role-taking, communication and related concepts simply serves to accentuate this point. [Emphasis added.]

Until recently, the relationship between emotions and the self was a relatively unexplored area. What came closest to analyzing the emotional component of the self was research on self-esteem (Rosenberg, 1979). However, through the work of interactionists (Shott, 1979; Averill, 1980; Gorden, 1981; Hochschild, 1983; Denzin, 1984b), we have begun to address directly the affective aspect of the self. This study takes seriously the affective component of the self.

As mentioned earlier, this study examines both the men's and women's interpretations of themselves and the other. For the most part, the men's and women's viewpoint in a relationship is compared. However, sometimes it will be necessary to take the individuals out of their relationship. Then, the analysis moves to an individual level. For example, the data show that when discussing how the men and women view their emotions, the men talk about their emotions in terms of control. The women do not make a direct reference to control. Therefore, to analyze the relationship between emotions and control, the focus is on the men's perspective. When examining behavior as in and out of control, however, the analysis focuses more on comparing the men's and women's perspectives.

Emotions as Out of Control

THE MEN'S EMOTIONS

The batterers often mentioned their inner feelings during the interviews. When they referred to their emotions in terms of their violence, they all spoke of feeling as if their anger or temper was out of control. For example, in our initial interview when Ronald discussed what he hoped to accomplish as part of the male batterer's group, he couched it in terms of control, "So, hopefully, through all this program, if I get in, I'll be able to sort out first of all, *how to control my own anger*." [Emphasis added.] Bill said in our first interview:

Did John explain to you that I've been in touch with fighting abuse in relationships? Like I'm in one now that's not abusive to the violent point. It's verbally, it's abusive, but I feel myself going back into where my *temper just gets to the point where it's out of control again* and what I was trying to do by getting into the group is being able to do something else with that anger instead of acting on it. [Emphasis added.]

Mike indicated this in our initial interview (the interviewer's remarks are in brackets):

[And what happened after the violent episode? Like how did you respond?] Scared and worry. I went for therapy over temper not too long after that. Trying to learn to *control temper.* [Emphasis added.]

When I first met with Kevin, he remarked:

I've got a quick temper. When someone defies me, my temper goes from 0 to 100 in about two milliseconds. It's just, I'm there. And once I get there, I'm dangerous. And I say dangerous in the sense of, if the person doesn't back down, we're going to end up with a confrontation. And if the confrontation goes long enough, it could end up with a bit of violence in it. I was talking to her I guess a couple of nights ago and I told her that I realized that was the problem, she was right about it. But that it had always been my anger in what had made me strong. And, *until I had learned to control that emotion*, I'm not really very safe to be around. [Emphasis added.]

Kevin's excerpt reveals that the interactive setting, specifically whether or not Kevin interprets Lisa's behavior as challenging his authority, influences whether or not he will "lose his temper" and use violence. Lisa verifies challenging Kevin's authority in our third interview:

I kept bucking his authority . . . I kept just not allowing any compromise at all . . . I just wouldn't yield to what he was asking . . . It's what I'm doing to communicate . . . I'm challenging his position . . . [it's] a challenge to his territory.

Thus, we see here a second facet of "feeling out of control." It is often influenced by the actor's interpretation of another's behavior (Athens, 1977, 1980, 1986; Denzin, 1984b).

When the women discuss their partner's emotions, they did not directly mention the issue of control. They would, for example, indicate that their mate may be unhappy or depressed, but they did not directly describe the men's feelings as uncontrollable. For example, Kay said this in our second interview:

I don't think he felt very much of himself because he wasn't really working . . . he would get in these moods where he'd be mopey and sit around all day and just, "I don't feel like going out. I just don't feel like it. I'm too depressed."

The women did not discuss the men's emotions as lived experiences. That is, they inferred how their mate felt based on how he behaved, but they did not discuss the batterers emotions as a subjective experience in terms of control or violence in the way that the men did. This reflects the different roles the men and women assume as perpetrator or victim in the violent interaction. Because the men directly experience the feeling that their emotions are uncontrollable, it makes sense that they would make a direct reference to control. The women cannot directly experience their partner's emotions; at best, they can make an inference regarding the emotional state of their partner based on how he behaves. The women do refer to the men feeling depressed or unhappy but these perceptions are based on external cues.

THE WOMEN'S EMOTIONS

Neither the men nor the women discuss the women's emotions in terms of control. In fact, the batterers make very little reference to how the women feel. This suggests that the men have low role-taking ability (Turner, 1969).[1] They typically do not put themselves in their mate's position and imagine how they feel. If they imaginatively adopted the position of their mate, they might not use violence. For example, in my third interview with

---

[1] The batterers may have low role-taking ability in the same way that rape assailants do not take the role of the other (Franks, 1985).

Kevin, I asked him what he thought made men come to the point of stopping their violence. He replied:

When I was sorry about the fact that I had gotten in a fight with Lisa, I wasn't really sorry that I had hurt her or that I had caused fear and pain and had suppressed her . . . What I was sorry for was that I had again hit her and that I had to live with that guilt inside me as a result of my actions . . . Now this last time, I really came to the point of . . . I've got to be sorry for her, not for me. And I've got to want to quit because of her or what I'm doing to her and quit thinking of me . . . That's why I say, the first thing is, the man's got to be truly sorry for what he's doing . . . Not because of what it inflicts on himself, but for what he's doing to the people around him.

The women never refer to their emotions as out of their control. Instead, they merely describe their emotions in terms of anger at being hit, or fear of being the recipient of further violence. For example, Mike would often tell Kay how sorry he was after a violent incident took place. When I asked her how she felt when he apologized, she said, "I felt angry. I felt such anger. I'd just like to tear him apart. But you couldn't. It wasn't allowed. There were parents." Kay felt that it was socially unacceptable to respond to her partner's violence with violence. Social norms guided her response, and in turn, her response supported societal expectations that women are not to behave aggressively.

In sum, we see that neither the men or women discuss the women's emotions in terms of control. In fact, the men generally did not discuss how their mate was feeling at all, suggesting that they did not take the role of the other and adopt their perspective. Only when the men discuss their feelings regarding a violent incident are emotions seen as out of control.

Discussion on Emotions

How can we explain the batterers emotions as out of control, particularly when they are violent? First, let me provide a working understanding of emotion from a symbolic interactionist perspective.[2] Then, I will explain how the out-of-control-emotions argument may be understood in light of both the data and the interactionist perspective.

Interactionists hold that emotions arise from one's interpretation or definition of the situation (Shott, 1979; Hochschild, 1979; Averill, 1980).

---

[2] Some researchers call the symbolic interactionist approach to emotions a "social constructionist" stance (Kemper, 1981). Moreover, while there are many different theoretical positions one may take toward understanding emotions (Kemper, 1981; Gorden, 1987), I do not want to debate the validity of these positions here. Rather, I will only address the symbolic interactionist view of emotions because I see this perspective as able to best explain the findings in this research.

As Averill (1980) says, "The object of an emotion is dependent on an individual's appraisal of the situation" (p. 310). Emotions are constructed with regard to how one makes sense of a situation (Shott, 1979). The significance of this is that emotions are not purely biologically or physiologically based but rather are an emergent characteristic of social interaction. Emotions do not exist as an inherent feature of individuals but rather originate and are expressed in social interaction.

Interactionists view the expression of particular emotions as guided by social and cultural norms that exist in social situations (Shott, 1979; Hochschild, 1979; Averill, 1980). Hochschild (1979, 1983) indicates that we should view particular emotional expressions as being managed and guided by "feeling rules" that exist in social situations. Given the norms and rules of situations, we learn the type and degree of emotional expression that is acceptable. By engaging in such emotion work, we thereby suppress a certain amount of feeling. For example, we learn that it is appropriate to feel sorrow at a funeral and to express that sorrow, but that to be gay and joyous would certainly result in ridicule. Therefore, if we really felt gay and joyous, such feelings would have to be suppressed because the norms of the situation do not call for expression of these feelings. As another example, flight attendants learn to be friendly to their passengers in order to entice further customer sales. To do otherwise would result in criticism by employers, and continued unfriendliness may result in a loss of the attendant's job. Therefore, negative feelings must be suppressed given the norms of the situation. The point of Hochschild's argument is that we manage our emotional expressions.

Stearns and Stearns (1986) discuss how, during this century, society places restrictions on expressing emotions (particularly anger) within marriage. Societal norms (as portrayed in the media or through counselors' therapeutic approaches) generally support the view that expressing anger is appropriate as long as it is managed. Anger is not to result in quarrels or verbal abuse. It is acceptable to fight as long as it is done calmly and rationally. Anger that is "out of hand" is viewed negatively: "Angry people were bad people. For the marriage counselors, the key word was immaturity" (Stearns & Stearns 1986, p. 193). Conflict is expected to occur in marriage, but it is to be handled by controlling one's anger, talking things out, quickly resolving the problem, and getting on with developing a good marriage.

Why is anger in marriage supposed to be controlled? Stearns and Stearns argue that with the onslaught of industrialization, rationality and reason, which guided one's behavior at work, infiltrated behavior at home. People were viewed as immature if they could not control their feelings and adopt appropriate behaviors to conflict resolution. It is also important to note that during and after World War II, anger that was not controlled in the home was given the metaphor of a war. Individuals had recently experienced a war that had resulted in much human aggression. Unleashed anger in the home was dangerous because it was viewed as threatening civilized life as the war had threatened civilization.

Stearns and Stearns point out that for a brief period in the late 1960s and early 1970s, norms shifted to expressing anger without constraint in marriage. Part of this was due to a new ideology of feeling and acting on one's anger. However, Stearns and Stearns argue that though the controls on anger were lifted for a few years, limits were still set. Moreover, it never really significantly changed the deep-seated belief that one's full expression of anger is not good and hence is inappropriate.

This historical and sociological analysis of the norms guiding the expression of anger in marriage is particularly relevant to the present analysis. If men behave violently in a relationship, whether it be marriage or cohabitation, they are not following the norm of emotional expression that guides that situation. Instead of controlling their emotions, they are being quite permissive with them. It would appear that they know that they are not following the norm of emotional expression since the men indicate that their emotions are "out of control." Why don't they follow the norm of controlling emotions when they know that such a norm exists? It is possible that they have not learned how to.

As the airline industry may have to teach flight attendants how to manage their emotions by expressing them according to the norms of the situation, so too a batterer may need to be taught how to manage his emotions. The batterers may not have learned that while they can't control how they feel about others, they *can* control whether and how they act on those feelings. It is possible that some batterers learn this only through treatment. For example, in our second interview, Frank described what he had learned in therapy:

It brought me to the reality that she doesn't provoke me to hit her. I provoke myself by listening, standing, and building myself up to do this act. I control my actions and it brought me to that reality. No matter what happens, I can take two alternatives or more. Leave. Ignore it or deal with it. But never ever come to the conclusion to strike her. I made that decision and I alone. Not her.

Mike said in our last interview:

A lot of my different ideas though, before, violence was not a choice. I mean, it was automatic. Now I've taught myself that how I react and how I feel and everything that I do is my choice. I control what happens to me, and I am responsible for what happens. And so long as I can keep that attitude I don't see that there's ever going to be a problem again.

Frank indicates that participation in group therapy made him realize that he controls his own actions. Mike mentions that he has learned that he makes a choice to be violent and that he is responsible for the consequences of his behavior. It is possible that for some people, such realizations may never occur without therapeutic help.

There is an alternative way of understanding descriptions of emotions as out of control. Claiming that emotions are "out of control" may serve to absolve batterers of the full responsibility of their actions (Averill, 1976). Being "overcome by anger" is at once an interpretation of one's behavior, and at the same time an experience of passivity (Averill, 1980). It implies that the individuals had no self-control and that their behavior was not something they willingly chose to perform. They were overwhelmed by emotion and thus should not be held responsible.

Tavris argues that saying particular emotions are out of control provides both a rationale and excuse for behaving violently. If a batterer says his anger was out of control, anger is the reason to hurt the other, and the fact that it is out of control serves as an excuse for the violence:

Why do we resist the idea that we can control our emotions, that feeling angry need not inevitably cause us to behave violently? . . . Because they excuse us . . . James Averill notices that we do not abdicate responsibility for all of our emotions, just the negative ones. No one apologizes for being swept away by a tidal wave of kindness and donating five thousand dollars to a worthy cause. A bystander who intervenes to prevent an assault or mugging is unlikely to apologize for acting courageously. We want credit for our noble emotions and tolerance for our negative ones and losing one's temper, "misplacing" it in a fleeting hour of insanity, is the apology that begs such tolerance. While anger serves our private uses, it also makes our social excuses. (Tavris, 1982, pp. 61– 62)

Gorden (1981, 1987) also discusses emotions in terms of absolving oneself of responsibility. As he says, "In situations and relationships that we value in relation to self, we pursue credit for positive images, and seek to avoid responsibility for feelings and acts that generate negative images" (Gorden 1981, p. 588). Gorden (1987) suggests that employing the loss of control description for an emotion serves to indicate to others that it is not characteristic of the individual's "real self." This is similar to Denzin's argument. As he notes, "When people are charged with violent conduct, they may contend that it was not their 'real self' that was acting. They make an appeal to an inauthentic mode of being themselves" (Denzin 1984b, p. 177).

From research on 18 batterers, Ptacek (1985) finds that while the men *feel* out of control, when they describe their *behavior* there is evidence that they are in control. Therefore, Ptacek argues that batterers use the out-of-control-emotions argument as an excuse to absolve themselves of full responsibility. He notes that in our culture there is the belief that we cannot control how we express our anger, and batterers actively participate in this cultural misunderstanding with the result that they effectively disavow their deviance by denying responsibility for their behavior. Ptacek (1985) indicates that "the loss of control associated with anger in our culture is to a large extent socially constructed" (p. 109). Indeed, Tavris notes that in other cultures (for example, the Eskimos), one is expected to control himself when angry. Ptacek does not accept batterers' accounts at face value. He says that there is a self-serving motive behind what they say; to convince others and themselves that their behavior is not their fault.

Ptacek may be making a moral judgment on the men's accounts. What if the batterers have merely *learned* that anger leads to aggression? Ptacek does not rule out this possibility. Can we then infer a motive behind the violence? If the data do show that the batterers believe that what they have learned is employed when they are violent, it is difficult to infer any motive behind this belief unless there is evidence suggesting what that motive may be. At best, Ptacek's argument is based on speculation.

Therefore, two alternative interpretations can be offered for the out-of-control-emotions argument. On the one hand, the batterers may merely lack proper skills to manage their emotions; they may learn this only in therapy. On the other hand, the out-of-control argument may be used as a mechanism to absolve batterers of the full responsibility of their violent behavior. In this way emotions are not out of control, but respondents say they are in order to provide an account (Scott & Lyman, 1968) or motive (Mills, 1940; Perinbanayagam, 1977) for violent behavior.

Later, I will argue that neither of these interpretations is an appropriate way of understanding emotions as out of control when violence occurs. They ignore the complex and processual nature of the violent act and the different aspects of the self that intrude into domestic violence to produce and/or control it. I will show that emotions as "out of control" is a real part of the violent act in interaction. For now, let me turn to another research finding in this study, that is, descriptions of *behavior* as both in *and* out of the batterer's control.

Behavior as In and Out of Control

THE MEN'S BEHAVIOR

The men believe that because their emotions are out of control, it causes them to act in an impulsive way. They claim they are unaware of what they are doing. It is an irrational, involuntary response. Kevin said in our first interview:

Usually what happens though is that once I struck her or pushed her or whatever I did, it was like all of my frustration and anger went out through my body with whatever I did to her, and then I would just go from 100 down to mellow. And I didn't care what she said. I didn't care what the situation was. *I was rational again.* I could leave. [Emphasis added.]

By saying that he was "rational again," Kevin implies that he was irrational and out of control earlier. Doug remarked in our final interview, "And she got hit. To me, it was a knee jerk response to her last remark." Doug's remark that it was a "knee jerk response" indicates that his response was automatic and something over which he had no control. Both Kevin and Doug imply that violence is not something they willingly choose to perform.

The batterers may even adopt a passive stance, as when Doug notes that "she got hit." They may indicate that they do not actively participate in the violence as is illustrated in the following excerpt from my initial interview with Frank:

I found myself having my hand around her throat and just really just [inaudible] the shit out of her. And I said, "Hey. No." She's calling out to me, "You're choking me." And that's when I came back and realized what I was doing.

Frank, like the others, views himself as a passive onlooker to his own violence.

These findings seem to support Denzin's and Berkowitz's thesis that violence is unpredictable, impulsive, and uncontrollable. However, we need to examine violent behavior more closely and, more importantly, look deeper into respondents descriptions of the men's behavior. When I did this, I found that the notion of uncontrollable behavior did not fully characterize descriptions of the men's behavior.

Although the batterers view their violent behavior as out of control, there are a number of instances where it is clear they perceive their violent behavior as in their control. This apparent inconsistency is paralleled by the women's accounts. Some women would describe their partner's behavior as *both* in and out of control. Other women would indicate their partner's behavior as *either* in or out of their control. To gain an understanding of both the men's and women's variation in describing the men's behavior, the following examples are relevant. Ronald said in our first interview:

I mean, I've never bruised her or done any visible [harm].

In our third interview, however, he said this:

My rational mind was trying to be humane about it. However, then my [inaudible] would take over and I'd say, "I don't like this person now. Just get them the fuck out of my apartment. I don't care what their story is." And that's basically what happens any time you hit anybody or anything. It's like, obviously *your rational mind says, "Hey wait. This is just a person. Can't we work this out?"* La-dee-da. *But then you just go over the edge.* [Emphasis added.]

Kathy (Ronald's partner) said in our first interview:

So, it's almost like it was like *out of the blue.* I wouldn't know that it was coming. I mean, I knew we were angry at each other but I didn't think that it had reached that point. [Emphasis added.]

She noted early in our third interview that, "He was totally *out of control.* It was like living with a psychotic." [Emphasis added.] Later in the interview, she said:

So like maybe we would argue on Monday. Then, Wednesday, something would happen at work, and maybe we'd just be kind of not nice to each other or something. Well, Friday would come around, and then we'd get into it. And then like some other issue or something would come up, and I would say something and he would get really mad.

Although Ronald had indicated at one point that his behavior was controlled because he "never bruised her or did any visible damage, " later he says that his behavior was an irrational response. Kathy also gives different accounts. On the one hand, she indicates that Ronald's behavior was out of control. Later, however, she notes the predictability of the violence by indicating when she expected it to occur. Here, Kathy is describing past events, and while past events do not totally determine future events, they do influence them. The point is that she is indicating that, in the past, the violence was somewhat patterned and predictable and not totally impulsive.

Larry and Terri discussed the violence in this way. Larry said in our first interview:

I'd take this chair that was sort of falling apart, and it wasn't a blind thing cause I'd take it break it into pieces. I'd slam it on the floor. And my AA sponsor pointed out, "Larry if that was blind rage, you wouldn't have picked the only area in the whole room to slam it where it wasn't going to hurt anything." Right? There was that one piece of floor I could put it and he would say that, and I'd say, "Yeah, I guess you're right."

Then, in our second interview he said:

But we've addressed the escalation which [inaudible]. Everything from walking away to find some cue where you all of sudden feel like you're in the child part of a parent-child. Whatever it is you feel, when you notice that, and then they say, here's what you do and you have something that I'll say which is, "I don't want to talk about this any more." And then it's my responsibility when I'm all right with it to say, "Okay, I'm ready to talk about it."

Terri said in our second interview:

It seemed to be much more that *anything could spark him off* rather than talking about it. Touchy subject. It just kind of got very, very *unpredictable*, I guess. And it was the unpredictability that scared me, too. [Emphasis added.]

Larry agrees with his Alcoholics Anonymous sponsor that breaking the chair into pieces in a place where it could not hurt anyone was probably a controlled response. In all my interviews with Larry, he provided instances where he felt his behavior was controlled. However, Larry would also indicate that he was working on controlling his behavior when he got angry with Terri. Terri implies that Larry's behavior was uncontrollable by indicating it's unpredictability. This supports Larry's belief that he can't control his behavior when he is angry. However, it also contradicts Larry's belief that his behavior is controlled.

To give a further illustration, Frank and Nancy reported the following. In my first interview, Frank said:

And I would never beat her with my fist or anything like that. I'd always hit her with my open hand and slap her.

Nancy said in our first interview:

And I don't believe he blacks out. *I believe he knows everything he's doing.* Because he did mention the fact one time that he tries to scare me into telling him the truth even when I'm not lying to him. [Emphasis added.]

In our second interview, however, Nancy said:

I watch Frank fight now with his brother, and I know that he stops and he thinks about what he's going to do before he hits them. Like, I've never lost my temper to the point that I've wanted to hit someone. I've never lost my temper that bad. I mean, I've spanked my kids as discipline. But, it's not usually I'm so mad I'm going to beat them up. It's like, you deserve this, bend over. Whereas Frank will just lash out at them. But Frank premeditates. I can't explain what I mean. His eyes get this look in it. Okay, my kids even notice it. Mary calls it fire in his eyes. And Harry says his eyes get big. *And I say he's possessed.* I do. I swear to God I think that man is. Anyway, this man took psychology for four years. And he told me that he thought Frank was a paranoid schizophrenic. And he's the one who's religious. And I've been thinking about this a long time because I was raised, and I know pretty much what is going on. Because I'm not a Christian doesn't mean I don't know what's going on. Well, the feelings I get from Frank when he gets like that are evil. *I really believe Frank is possessed with demons.* I swear to God I do. I know you probably think that's crazy, but you don't know how he looks when he gets like that and his face goes white. He's black but his face, it turns a chocolate milk brown and his lips get real white, and his eyes get like this. I just can't explain it. [Emphasis added.]

Earlier I indicated that Frank would adopt a passive stance to his violence, thus suggesting that he did not willingly choose to perform the violence because he was not an active and voluntary participant. Here, however, he implies that his behavior was in control because he "would never beat her with my fist." Nancy also gives varying accounts on whether Frank's behavior was in his control. Though in our initial interview she notes that the violence was calculated, in our second interview she says that the violence was brought on by a "possessed" man.[3] This suggests that it was not her partner's "real self" that was acting but rather someone (or something) else.

The men and women are saying in different ways how the men's be-

---

[3] Nancy's use of the term "premeditation" suggests supporting evidence for Frank's behavior as in control. However, given the immediate context in which the term appears, it is difficult to understand how premeditation fits in with what she is saying. It is possible that she does not know what the word means and therefore uses it inappropriately.

havior was both in and out of their control. The different accounts suggest that violence is not totally uncontrollable as Berkowitz and Denzin would argue. Rather, sometimes violence is expected and at other times it is unexpected. As will be shown later, these different accounts may be understood in terms of the relationship between the different aspects of the self and the violent act, both of which are embedded in interaction.

THE WOMEN'S BEHAVIOR

Neither the men or women discussed the women's behavior as in or out of control. The men might discuss their mate's behavior in terms of, for example, the women provoking the violence, but their behavior was not described as controllable or uncontrollable. Similarly, the women would describe their own behavior by indicating, for example, that they would try to do things so as to please their mate and not upset him, but they did not discuss their own behavior in terms of control. Therefore, the issue of control only becomes relevant for respondents when describing the men's behavior.

Discussion on Behavior

The respondents provide different descriptions on the batterers' behavior in terms of control. It is unclear whether the varying accounts on behavior as in *and* out of control reflects (*a*) the respondents' confusion about the violence itself, (*b*) specific incidents which may be more spontaneous and uncontrolled than others, or (*c*) an underlying neutralization of a negative label.

With respect to the latter case, for example, whether respondents say the violence is in or out of the batterer's control may depend upon their viewing the effect of this account as neutralizing the "bad person" label. For the batterers, when they say that their behavior is out of control, they are implying that they were not really responsible for their actions and that they really are a good person. When they say that they had control, they suggest that they held back, that it could have been worse. Thus, they are not that bad a person. When a woman mentions the violence as unpredictable, she implies that neither the batterer nor herself is inherently bad. Rather, there is merely a problem with her partner controlling his anger. When she mentions the predictability of the violence, she suggests that though she may be involved with a bad person, she is not a bad person herself. It is not her fault and perhaps she deserves some sympathy.

The men and women are saying in different ways that the men's behavior was both in and out of their control. On the one hand, the men indicate that their behavior was out of control by mentioning how the violence was an impulsive or irrational response. On the other hand, they discuss their behavior as in their control by noting that the damage they did could have been worse. As with the issue of emotions discussed earlier, it is the batterers who *directly* feel their behavior is impulsive or know that they had the capacity of inflicting more injury but stopped short of that. The women cannot directly experience what their partners feel when they behave violently; they cannot experience the impulsiveness or sense the possibility of hitting harder but holding back. They can only experience the behavior that is actually enacted.

The women describe their partners' behavior in terms of control in a more *indirect* way. If the violence was viewed as unpredictable, then it implied that the batterer had no control over his actions. When they viewed the violence as predictable, this suggests that their partner had some control. In addition, they might mention that their partner knew exactly what he was doing, again implying that he had control over his behavior.[4]

The women's perception of their partners' behavior as unpredictable is similar to the men's perception of their behavior as impulsive. Neither the men nor the women are indicating that the men's behavior, in general, is unpredictable because we all want to believe that our behavior, on the whole, is consistent or that we are involved with a person whose behavior is fairly consistent. Rather, they are both saying, but in different ways, that sometimes when violence occurs, it is unexpected.

If the batterers' behavior is out of their control, then should their behavior be characterized as impulsive? Berkowitz (1983) seems to think so. He argues that there are two types of human aggression: impulsive and instrumental. Impulsive aggression is behavior carried out primarily to injure another person. To injure is an end in itself. As Berkowitz (1983) says, "If we stop and think about it, it is only a matter of common sense that angry people want to hurt those who had provoked them" (p. 174). This type of aggression is an involuntary response. Instrumental aggression is behavior that primarily is directed beyond injury and "in the pursuit of nonharmful objectives" (Berkowitz, 1983, p. 173), for example, control. It is a more calculated, planned behavior.

Berkowitz does not deny that violence may sometimes be explained as an attempt to control the victim's actions. However, he argues that much human aggression occurs in the "heat of strong emotions" and that sociologists should look at aggression as being more impulsive than calculated (Berkowitz, 1983, p. 179). Applying this belief to wife-beating, he suggests that we view the self as driven by anger with the result that the self acts violently but in an involuntary manner. Denzin (1984b) shares this view in that he characterizes domestic violence as the self responding emotionally and in an uncontrollable fashion.

---

[4] It should be pointed out that the women sometimes used the term "out of control" to describe their partner's violent behavior, for example, Kathy's excerpt cited earlier. In this sense, there was a direct reference to control.

On the surface, the argument by Berkowitz and Denzin appears valid, especially when one looks at how the batterers felt during a violent incident. However, it is useful to examine the issue more closely. If, as Berkowitz argues, violence is not premeditated and is enacted only with the goal of injuring the other, then it is essential to determine whether or not this goal is present when violence begins. One way to determine the presence of this goal would be to ask the respondents what made the batterers stop their violence once it was underway. If they respond that it would end when the batterers felt that they had hurt their partners, then such evidence would support the notion of impulsivity.

In his thesis, Ptacek discusses the intent to injure in some detail. He directly asked the batterers if they intended to hurt their wives or lovers. He does not find overwhelming support for this goal. In fact, he finds that there is more evidence that the batterers had as their goal not the intent to injure, but the intent to control their partners, which would support a more instrumental than impulsive aggression. However, Ptacek's argument is flawed on two counts. First, and most importantly, he asked the batterers if they *intended to hurt their partners* rather than asking them *what made them stop the violence once it was underway*. Second, according to Berkowitz, the intent to injure does not occur prior to or following a violent incident but rather during a violent act itself. Therefore, Ptacek's test of the intent to injure is incorrect simply because he is examining whether or not the intent is there prior to the violence or present after the violence (when the batterers reflect upon why they were violent). Certainly, Berkowitz's work is ambiguous as far as determining when the intent to injure exists, which suggests that there is need for further clarification of this issue.

Although it is argued that testing the intent to injure requires determining what made the batterer stop his violence at a particular point, the present data cannot capture this because the issue of intent was seen as relevant only after the data were collected. Future research is needed to directly address this issue.

There are two opposing explanations for why a batterer's behavior may be viewed as out of control. On the one hand, Berkowitz and Denzin argue that behavior is out of control due to the impulsive nature of violence toward women. On the other hand, Ptacek challenges the impulsivity of violence and argues that it should be viewed more in instrumental terms. He finds ample evidence to indicate that the man's violence is directly related to a desire to control his partner.

Summary

This chapter has revealed that emotions are viewed as out of control and behavior is viewed as in and out of control when the batterers are violent. Several different explanations have been offered for these findings. The position I take in this research is that we must go beyond analyzing descriptions of the violence in terms of a lack of managing emotions, avoiding responsibility, or averting a negative label. Furthermore, conceptualizing violence in impulsive terms as do Berkowitz and Denzin or in instrumental terms as does Ptacek is also inadequate. These explanations assume that violence can be understood on an individual level by attempting to explain why a batterer is violent. Violence, however, is a function of both the man's and woman's actions and reactions and thus must be understood within an interactive framework. In short, the dynamics of violence are much more complex than any of these perspectives permit.

In order to examine the complexity of violence, we must examine it processually. The symbolic interactionist perspective is particularly relevant in this endeavor. As I will show, the views that emotions are out of control and behavior is in and out of control when one is violent are understood in terms of the relationship between the different aspects of the self and the violent act, both of which are embedded in interaction. Let me turn now to that explanation.

5
Explaining Violence in Terms of Control

In this chapter, I will show how the symbolic interactionist perspective can be used in order to understand the relationship between emotions, behavior, control and violence as it emerges in reflective thought and in interaction. In doing this, I examine the complex and processual nature of the violent act as it exists in interaction. Additionally, I address the different aspects of the self, that is, the "I" and "Me" that intrude into the violent act to produce and/or control it.

I will begin by identifying the violent act as comprising four stages and then show how they relate to the different components of the self, control and violence. These stages and the role that the "I" and "Me" play in the act are grounded in Meadian thought and form the basis for understanding the relationship between control and violence. Certainly, this is not all there is to domestic violence, but it provides a starting point for understanding the dynamics of violence in interaction.

Given the respondent's descriptions of the violence, I attempt to generate a theory of the interactive processes embedded within the violent act. I will show that being in *and* out of control can co-exist, that violence can be understood in both impulsive and instrumental terms, especially when we examine the violence over time. Let me turn, first, to identifying the stages of the violent act.

An Interactionist Perspective

Mead indicated that all human behavior that is not habitual is built up in the process of execution; human action is constructed as it goes along (Meltzer, 1978). The significance of this is that humans not only react but, more importantly, act. Mead's conceptualization of the *act* of an individual and the relevance of the phases of the self (the "I" and "Me") for the act is important towards understanding violence in terms of control.

Mead (1938) identified an act as having four general stages: impulse, perception, manipulation, and consummation. These stages describe the processual nature of an act during interaction. Continually alternating and intruding into the act (Mead, 1938) are the "I," the self as subject, the part of the self acting spontaneously and without reflective thought, and the "Me," the self as object, the part of the self that is reflective and holds the organized attitudes of others (Wiley, 1979; Bolton, 1981). Violence must first be understood in terms of its construction by way of the stages of the violent act during interaction.[1]

The impulse stage is the first of these four stages and it appears when a problematic situation exists, "a lack of adjustment between the individual and his world" (Mead 1938, p. 6). The presence of a stimulus, from which the problematic situation arises, prompts an attitude to the stimulation "which is that of the reaction of the individual to the stimulation" (Mead 1938, p. 3). This reaction is an initial, subjective, spontaneous, and non-reflective response. Of the two components of the self, the "I" and the "Me," the aspect of the self that responds in this stage is the "I."

The perception stage follows as an object becomes the focus of attention and calls forth action with reference to it (Mead, 1938). An individual at once plans possible lines of action to complete the act and perceives an object that invites possible action toward it in order to successfully complete the act. In this stage, the "Me" dominates and guides the "I" towards completion of the act.

The manipulation stage takes place after the perception stage. In this stage, a person carries out conduct that was only thought about in the prior stage. An individual experiences contact with the object and acts with reference to it. The "I" dominates and under the direction of the "Me" carries out the impulse. The perception and manipulation stages are indicative of the interplay between the "I" and "Me." In general, the "Me" helps shape and direct the actions of the "I" in these two stages.

Consummation is that last stage and it occurs when the impulse is carried out (Mead, 1938). It is the completion of the act. This prompts the "Me" part of the self into an evaluation of the act, which is an interpretive process. All acts begin with the "I" and end with the "Me."

Violence, a human action, must be understood in terms of its construction by way of the stages of the act. Before examining this construction, let me discuss particular contextual cues that prompt the first stage of the violent act, thereby setting the process of violence into motion. I asked all respondents to indicate what led to violent incidents and was later able to identify several patterns. First, when a woman's behavior was *perceived* by the man as challenging to his power, decisions, authority, or control,

---

[1] Denzin (1984b) uses the Meadian act to explain the relationship between interpretation and understanding. My application of the Meadian act to domestic violence parallels his application of the Meadian act to the hermeneutic circle of interpretation and understanding.

violence often erupted. For example, Mike said in our second interview:

> I wouldn't let her [Kay] see her friends. I wouldn't let her go do things she needed to be doing. . .I guess the only way that I could get her back in line was to hit her. . . It's a control situation.

Kay verifies Mike's control in our second interview when she said:

> If I decided to cut my hair and went ahead and did it, I would get into a lot of trouble. . . If I'd go to the grocery store and I'd take a little bit longer than what I should have, he didn't like it because I wasn't supposed to do anything that I wasn't told to do.

Here, the reference to control is not how the man feels or behaves, but rather whether or not he successfully controls his partner. Although the former has an internal reference (control of oneself), the latter has an external reference (control of the other).[2] Moreover, we see how societal expectations influence the eruption of violence. Since men are expected to have power, they may resort to physical means to reassert themselves if they believe that power is being threatened.[3]

A second catalyst that often influenced violent episodes was finances. Many of the respondents said that arguments over money would inevitably lead to violence. In general, both individuals in the relationship were aware that this was a cue that violence might arise. It appeared that conflict arose regarding spending habits of one or both partners. Therefore, although money matters was a separate issue, it still had the underlying element of control.

A third cue was friendships with others that often caused jealousy on one or both partner's part. When friendships were with persons of the opposite sex, problems arose regarding fidelity. Many of the respondents mentioned that when they suspected that their partner was seeing someone else and confronted them about it, it often led to violence. Again, both individuals

---

[2] Athens (1977, 1980, 1986) indicates that there are four situations in which violent acts are committed. These include the physically defensive, frustrative, malefic (the victim belittles the actor and the actor interprets the victim as evil or malicious), and frustrative malefic (the victim blocks the actor's goal and the victim is viewed as malicious) type. A careful examination of Athens' own examples, however, reveals that embedded in each of these situations is the issue of control. For example, in the frustrative situation, control operates because the victim is viewed as resisting the actor's line of action and the actor responds to this resistance by being violent. Therefore, when examining violent behavior, it is the issue of control that is particularly relevant.

[3] Another example of the use of power to control in interaction is shown in Kollock et al. (1985). Those who interrupt others in conversations are more likely to be powerful persons and these are more likely to be men. Therefore, certain behaviors are associated with more powerful individuals in situations of control.

in the relationship were aware that the issue of fidelity influenced violence.

Same-sex friendships also caused problems. Specifically, a woman's female friends had a tendency to influence violent episodes. The women indicated that they inevitably lost the majority of their female friends after they had met their partner. In one relationship, the man's male *and* female friends sometimes caused problems. Kathy mentioned that when Ronald would go out with his friends, she sometimes got upset because he was not spending enough time with her. When they would discuss the issue later, it would often develop into an argument, with Ronald sometimes behaving violently. Despite Kathy's unhappiness with Ronald's friends, Ronald persisted in seeing his friends and never lost any of them.

Although cross-sex or same-sex friendships was a separate issue that influenced violent episodes, it still had the underlying element of control. One or both partners felt threatened and jealous when the other went out with a male or female friend. As a result of these feelings, violence often erupted.

The issue of control serves to bring forth an initial, spontaneous impulse to aggress on the part of the batterer. The batterer's "I," his subjective and nonreflective aspect of himself, responds. The woman stands out as a distant object (the target) in the perception stage. The batterer focuses attention on her and decides upon a line of action with reference to her. The "Me" (the expectations others have about us regarding how we are to act) is called forth in the construction of the violence and thereby gives direction to the "I." Because men are socialized to be aggressive, especially when situations of conflict arise, and because they generally are not punished for behaving aggressively toward women (Dobash & Dobash, 1979), they may view violent conduct as an appropriate response, especially when conflict over control arises. Their conduct depends upon the nature of the "Me."

After the perception stage, the manipulation stage takes place. The specific form of violence that is planned in the perception stage is now administered by the "I." For example, if a man "planned" to beat up his wife in the perception stage, he would carry out this violence in the manipulation stage.

The last stage, consummation, occurs when the violence has ended and the impulse to aggress has been acted out. The "Me" reappears to interpret the situation and evaluates whether or not the act has been completed. Therefore, all acts begin with the "I" and end with the "Me." If the violence is interrupted in the course of its execution either by the police or neighbors, it is possible that the impulse to aggress has not been released and the act has not been completed.

Therefore, violence must first be examined on a micro level and placed within the basic framework of the act. Let me now examine additional processes and features that occur during the execution of violence and following the completion of the act.

FIGURE 5.1. A symbolic interactionist model of domestic violence.*

Impulse	Perception	Manipulation	Consummation	Post Consummation
	Expectation of "Me" to be:	3. Carry out impulse (proceed as planned)	Act ends	Guilt
	1. Violent			
Problematic situation arises**		4. Check impulse (proceed, but with control)	Act ends	Controlled the violence
	2. Nonviolent			
		5. Inhibit aggression	Act ends	

(E, F, C, D, A, B paths shown with arrows between Violent/Nonviolent and the Manipulation options)

*Solid Arrows: More likely paths
 Broken Arrows: Less likely paths
**Conflict over control

PERCEPTION

The perception stage, the point at which the woman becomes the object for the batterer's aggression, is a critical juncture in the act because the content of the "Me" influences whether one will plan violent conduct. The "Me," the organized attitudes of others held in the self of the person (Mead, 1934), are different for different people and change over time. The influence of the "Me" in the perception stage is similar to the arguments by Athens (1977, 1980, 1986) and Denzin (1984b) that one takes the attitude of the generalized other when interpreting a situation and deciding whether to behave violently.

The nature of the "Me" in the perception stage is violent or nonviolent in nature (1 and 2 in Figure 5.1). A violent "Me" may result from childhood such as witnessing or experiencing violence when young, or interpreting the expectations of others (others who may or may not be participants in the current situation) as calling for violent behavior. A nonviolent "Me" may arise from having learned that aggression is an inappropriate response to conflict or by interpreting others' expectations as calling for nonviolent conduct.[4]

---

[4] This is not to say that an individual's own interpretation of the situation has no bearing on the plan of action, for indeed these are also part of the "Me."

MANIPULATION

In the manipulation stage, one can either carry out the impulse to aggress (*3* in Figure 5.1), carry out the impulse but with some control (see *4*) or inhibit the impulse to aggress (see *5*). The present data suggest that it is more likely that inhibiting the impulse to aggress will occur when the expectations of the "Me" are to be nonviolent (Path *A* in Figure 5.1), and that Path *B* would occur infrequently. In the latter case, inhibiting the impulse to aggress could occur because the expectations of the "Me" do not totally influence behavior. Other factors, such as the situation or presence of other actors may more directly influence one's response. Therefore, such factors may override the expectations of the "Me."

I have noted that the respondents were inconsistent about the batterer's behavior being in or out of their control. This inconsistent testimony can be understood if we realize that the manipulation stage which is normally under the control of the impulsive "I" can be monitored by the "Me" to a greater or lesser degree. With respect to respondents' different accounts regarding whether or not the batterers' behavior is in their control, the "Me" may interrupt the actions of the "I" (during manipulation) and batterers become reflectively aware of their violence. Therefore, the impulse to aggress becomes monitored (*4* in Figure 5.1).[5] When the expectations of the "Me" are to be violent, the impulse to aggress may be partially controlled (Path *C*). Given the findings in this study, however, it is much more likely that when the expectations are to be nonviolent, the impulse is controlled (Path *D*). In either case, this interruption of the (uncontrolled) "I" by the (controlled) "Me" would explain respondent's accounts of the batterer's behavior as controlled.[6]

The batterers might proceed toward violence but do so with control because they realize that they could inflict severe damage. Deciding that this is not their intent, they may inflict less severe injury. Alternatively, they may anticipate feeling guilty about the physical damage they intend to inflict and want to avoid this feeling to some degree. Using control minimizes guilt feelings.

For some batterers and at some times, the "Me" does not interrupt the actions of the (uncontrolled) "I" in the manipulation stage, and the impulse to aggress is carried out (*3* in Figure 5.1). This is most likely to occur for those whose expectations of the "Me" are to be violent (Path *E*). However, for some, though the expectations of the "Me" are to be nonviolent, violent impulsive behavior is still enacted (Path *F*). This is possible

---

[5]This would be in line with Turner's (1976) notion of an institutionally based self.

[6]Whether or not the "Me" interrupts the actions of the "I" may also be a function of the ongoing interaction. Individuals may become aware of their behavior only when another draws it to their attention, resulting in the intrusion of the "Me." This is similar to the process of using individuals' names in an episode of collective action to refocus their attention to their "self" and disengage them from the mob scene (Diener, 1979; Prentice-Dunn & Rogers, 1982).

in instances where men, in settings such as a male battering program, may be learning (for the first time) the inappropriateness of violence against women. In such instances, enacting behavior that is in line with new attitudes may lag behind actual attitude change. In either case, this would explain respondent's accounts of the batterer's behavior as out of control. The batterer might carry out the impulse to aggress without interruption from the "Me" because his response has become habitual.[7]

CONSUMMATION

Finally, the evaluation of the act that results from carrying out the impulse to aggress may involve feelings of guilt, while the evaluation of the act following a check of the impulse may be more representative of having controlled the violence. The data in the present study does not fully capture the nature of consummation because I did not ask the batterers how they felt immediately after an incident. Instead, I asked about the *behavioral* reactions of each partner immediately following the incident. Future research needs to examine this feature of the model more directly. Evidence from the data, however, as illustrated in the next chapter, reveals that consummation seems to be operating in the manner described.

Given the different options that may be taken in the manipulation stage, it is not possible to specify the exact form of violence all batterers will employ in these different alternatives. This is because each batterer has a different set of experiences and attitudes that guides his behavior. For one, proceeding as planned might mean slapping his partner several times; for another, it might mean beating her up. Proceeding but controlling the violence for one may mean hitting with an open hand (slapping) and not the fist (punching); for another, it may mean giving the woman a black eye but not causing her to lose her eye. Moreover, how they behave also depends on the development of an interactive episode and the actions of the other.

It is important to note from the above that over time, violent acts may increase in severity, but for different reasons. On the one hand, a batterer may believe that while his violence at T1 released his impulse to aggress and enabled him to obtain his desired end, he may not believe that this same violence will achieve his desired end at T2. Therefore, he may use a higher level of violence to again release his impulse and obtain adequate rewards. In T1 and T2, the impulse to aggress has been released, but the nature of the impulse is more severe in T2. On the other hand, violence in T1 may have been more indicative of controlling (rather than releasing) the impulse to aggress. In T2, the batterer may release the impulse without control, resulting in increased violence. Therefore, the violence increases, but only because the earlier violence was put in check and the later violence was not.

---

[7] This would be in line with Turner's (1976) notion of an impulsively based self.

EMOTIONS AS OUT OF CONTROL AND BEHAVIOR AS IN AND OUT OF CONTROL

In order to address the batterers' accounts of their emotions and behavior as out of control, we need to examine the act in terms of the impulse to aggress. When the batterers say their emotions are out of control, I would argue that they are reflecting upon the entire act primarily in terms of the impulse to respond aggressively. If the "Me" interrupts conduct in the manipulation stage, they are more specifically reflecting upon the act prior to this interruption.

Descriptions of the violence as out of control in terms of emotions, and in or out of control in terms of behavior, can co-exist. While the violent act may be set in motion with the impulse to aggress (through the "I"), it may be carried out and completed with some degree of control (through the "Me"). Here, emotions would be viewed as out of control and behavior would be viewed as in control. If the impulse to aggress is carried out without interruption from the "Me" in the manipulation stage, then the view that emotions and behavior are out of control would appear. Therefore, the violent act, upon reflection, has both uncontrollable (impulsive) and controllable (instrumental) elements.

An additional point must be made. All of the respondents noted that a goal of the violence was to *control the women's behavior*. This will be discussed in greater detail in Chapter 7. Violent acts occur at a given point and reoccur over time. I would argue that the immediate consequence of the violent act is to satiate the impulse to aggress. When reflecting on the violence, the focus is on the uncontrollable nature of the act. For those who change from a violent to a nonviolent person, it is possible that when violence is reflected upon, the focus is more on how the nature of the act is controllable, both in terms of one's emotions and behavior.

The long-term consequence of the violence is to control the women's behavior. In the beginning, these long-term results may be unexpected or unintended. However, it is possible that, over time and through the process of learning, the act of violence is primarily carried out in order to control. The violence continues especially if the batterers do not experience negative consequences from it. It may be that an act that is originally impulsive in nature becomes, over time and through learning, an instrumental act carried out for other purposes.

Summary

This chapter has provided an analysis of the relationship between control and violence. The interactionist model that was generated incorporates both the reported uncontrollable and controllable nature of violence. Both the uncontrollable and controllable elements of violence exist in the model, given that the "I" and "Me" constantly alternate and/or intrude into the violent act. To a certain extent, the "I" and "Me" may be characterized as having an impulsive and instrumental flavor, respectively. The violent act can be viewed as having the immediate situational consequences of satiating the impulse to aggress, and the long-term learning consequences of controlling the other's behavior. Over time, impulsive violence may become instrumental violence.

When violence occurs, respondents view the batterers' emotions as out of control and their behavior as both in and out of control. The symbolic interactionist perspective was employed to explain this complexity of violence. Violence is a function of the self, especially the nature of the "Me" that the person has. In turn, the "Me" is a function of past experiences, including childhood as well as the current interactive situation, and including how significant others view the self.

The violent act consists of four general stages that are guided by the "I" and the "Me." The early part of the violent act is instigated by the "I" in correspondence with the type of "Me" that an individual has at the time. Expectations of the "Me" to be violent or nonviolent influence whether one will carry out the impulse to aggress, check the impulse to aggress, or inhibit aggression. If the "Me" interrupts the actions of the "I" during manipulation of the violence, then a batterer will check the impulse to aggress. If the "Me" does not interrupt the actions of the "I," the batterer will carry out the impulse to respond violently. This explains the respondent's descriptions of the batterer's behavior as both in and out of his control.

Respondents in this study attempted to make sense of their violence and describe it to me. My understanding of the violence has to do both with the underlying process of violence (including the stages of the violent act that is embedded in interaction, and the nature of the "I" and "Me") and with the sense-making of the respondents (including their use of the control notion). Domestic violence researchers need to more closely address what respondents say about the violence and see how this is associated with theoretical notions about violence.

The interactionist model resolves competing explanations that domestic violence is not controlled and impulsive and that violence is controlled and instrumental by showing the conditions under which each is true. By using the symbolic interactionist perspective, I attempted to describe the complex, processual, interactive nature of domestic violence. How the model specifically operates, given the data in this study, is addressed in Chapter 6. It is important to point out that the model that was presented should *not* be interpreted as describing only the batterer's behavior and thus be viewed as an individual model. Though the women's behavior is not explicitly incorporated into the model, it is present implicitly. The women affect the batterer's behavior. The interactive components of the model will be discussed in greater detail in Chapter 6.

6
Control as Object: Evidence for the Symbolic Interactionist Model

Chapter 5 presented a symbolic interactionist view of the relationship between violence and control. The model was presented to explain how violence can have both uncontrollable and controllable elements. This chapter provides detailed evidence from the data on how the model operates. Before presenting the findings, several preliminary remarks need to be made. These include clarifying what the model represents, discussing the shortcomings of the data, and identifying the subset of data that is used in the findings.

Clarifying the Model

Given what the respondents in this sample said about the violence, the model was presented as a way of summarizing how control relates to violence. When the respondents reflected upon the violence and tried to make sense of it, control was a meaningful object. The interactionist model was not generated to *predict* but rather to *describe* violence in relationships. For example, the model was not formulated so as to predict whether or how violence will be carried out given the expectations of the "Me," but rather was created to indicate what respondents see as relevant when behaving as they do. While it is possible to use the model to predict the probability and nature of violence (degree of control) in relationships, that was not its original purpose.

The model specifically addressed the men's use of violence in terms of the stages of the act. How the women felt and acted in a violent relationship was not explicitly incorporated into the model. If the women were the aggressors in the relationships, then the model could have been applied to them. However, because they were the recipients of violence in these relationships, the model was applied directly to the men.

Finally, the model summarized the relationship between control and violence given what the *men* rather than the *women* said. To a certain degree, the women's perspectives are relevant because, for example, their reports of the men's behavior being both in and out of their control support the men's contradictory statements of their behavior as also in and out of their control. However, for the most part, and as will be shown in this chapter, the women do not discuss the notion of control (in the way that the model relates it to violence) as the men do.[1]

Shortcomings to the Data

As noted earlier, this study was exploratory. As a result, when gathering the data, I did not have in mind collecting information that would enable me to support or disconfirm the interactionist model developed in the prior chapter. Rather, the model was generated only after analyzing the respondents' comments about the violence. Given their descriptions, I found that previous perspectives in domestic violence research were inadequate in explaining the respondents' reflections and that it was the symbolic interactionist framework that best fit the data.

Though the data to be discussed in this chapter will help explain, in greater detail, how the model operates by drawing on the respondents' descriptions of specific violent incidents, this data may not be as convincing as if I had asked relevant questions to directly tap into different aspects of the model. For example, I did not ask the respondents how they thought others expected the man to act at the time particular violent incidents occurred. This might have clarified the expectations of the "Me" in the perception stage. Rather than asking respondents how much control they felt the man had over the form of violence used during specific incidents, I merely asked the form of violence that was used. The former might indicate whether manipulation was more characteristic of carrying out or checking the impulse to aggress, while the latter could not tap into the nature of the manipulation. Finally, rather than asking respondents how the man felt immediately after an incident, I asked about the *behavioral* reactions immediately following an incident. The former might reveal the nature of consummation, upon reflection, while the latter could not do this.

In addition, in order to examine the relationship between control and the different stages of the violent act, it is important (and perhaps necessary) to get precise information on all violent incidents. This would enable one to examine whether or not the interactionist model holds for all violent incidents, and if it does not, how and when it departs. From my interviews with respondents, I found that it was difficult and sometimes impossible to

---

[1] The women do mention the notion of control, but they discuss it in terms of attempts by their partners to control them. This will be discussed in greater detail in Chapter 7.

obtain clear and detailed information on *all* the violent incidents. The lack of such information, despite my probing, may have been due to several things. It may have been emotionally difficult for the respondents to share all the violent incidents. Additionally, they may have wanted to preserve their self-esteem, either because they enacted violence against another or were the recipient of repeated violence. Not recounting all the incidents may have been a way to preserve their self-esteem. Finally, it may have been difficult to recall violent incidents that occurred years ago.

The data that are used in the findings are discussed below. Two questions are answered. First, what kind of violent incidents form the basis of the interactionist model? Second, what respondents generally describe these incidents?

Identifying the Subset of Data

To analyze the relationship between control and violence, the data were examined in the following way. First, I recorded all incidents in which it was clear that some form of violence was used against the women. These incidents were either detailed or general in nature. In the former, the respondents would usually indicate when the violence occurred, what appeared to precipitate the violence, what form of violence was used, and how each partner responded to the incident, that is, the behavioral reactions immediately following the incident. In the latter case, the respondents typically indicated that violence occurred and noted the form of violence used, but they did not provide detailed information such as when or why the violence was used. The following is an example of these two types of incidents from my first interview with Kathy. The first part of the excerpt reveals Kathy's detailed description of a violent episode. In the latter part of the excerpt, Kathy provides a more general description of the violence she experienced:

There was two in the same night that I can remember. [When was this?] This was sometime in September or October. I don't remember, but I know I was taking karate for awhile, and I had sparred once so I felt what it was like to fight with somebody. I had never fought before. I was really mad at him about something about Mark and Joan again. I went to his room and said something to him, and then I think he started hitting me so I finally started hitting him back. I was punching him and stuff. I was like totally outraged that I would have been brought to do this. And I had never hit anyone, ever. And I never wanted to, and here I was hitting somebody, and then I finally just went into my room, and I cried, and I was hysterical, and then I was mad at myself for having to cry because I thought I had finally mastered anger, and I didn't have to cry anymore. But there I was crying and, oh, it was just a terrible scene. So then Ronald came in and was being very soothing. I don't remember what happen then, but I guess I wasn't ready to forgive him whatever because we started fighting again, and it was pretty much about the same issue, and then he like pushed me, and my head knocked against the wall, and that's when he like started choking me or something like that. And, I was like totally drained from having fought him before that I was so sore that I just laid there and started crying again. . . . [Can you recall anything other than that?] Yes, I can. There was one time where he threw, like we were cooking something, and he just like threw the pan up in the air in the kitchen on me. There was another time when he punched a hole in my wall. Oh, there might have been one time where he actually hit me. I think he was like punching me or something like that.

In total, the respondents discussed 73 violent incidents in detail and 20 general violent incidents. The men mentioned 31 violent incidents in detail and 10 general violent incidents, and the women discussed 42 incidents in detail and 10 general incidents. It is not surprising that the women discussed more incidents than the men. The batterers would probably experience more guilt than the women by sharing all the violent incidents. Admitting that one was violent was probably much more difficult than admitting one was the recipient of violence.

When comparing the men's and women's descriptions of violent incidents in detail, I found that the notion of control was discussed in 52% ($N = 16$) of the incidents mentioned by the batterers, although none of the women discussed control when describing incidents in detail. For example, Larry and Terri gave different descriptions of the same violent incident in my first interview with each of them. Larry said:

Probably 12 or 13 weeks at one point, I left the house in the middle of one of these things, and before I did I grabbed her by the shoulders, and I was just enraged, I was just insensitive. And I grabbed her, and I shook her, and I told her I was leaving because what I wanted to do was smash her face, and that's what I wanted to do.

Terri said:

I think one time, I don't remember when it was, but one time this spring, he grabbed me by the shoulders and was shaking me. We were arguing about something, screaming into my face or something, I don't know. And I again I got really scared.

Larry indicates that he proceeded to be violent (grabbing her shoulders and shaking her), but he used some control because what he really wanted to do was "smash her face." Terri makes no mention of Larry using any control. She only indicates what she experienced.

It should be pointed out that Larry *indirectly* rather than *directly* mentions control in the above excerpt. My interpretation of what he says is thus based on what I think Larry is implying. When the data in this study were coded, many indirect references to control appeared. Therefore, not only respondents' explicit use of the term control but also their implicit reference to it served to represent the code, "control."

Therefore, when the respondents reflect on particular violent acts, it is the batterer, not the victim, who views control as relevant. This supports the fact that the model explains the relationship between violence and control from the perspective of the aggressor as opposed to the victim. Given that the interview style was semistructured and open-ended, it is rather surprising that such a large proportion of the incidents mentioned by the men were discussed in terms of control.

The findings presented in this chapter examine those instances where the men discussed the notion of control in order to see how it forms the basis of the interactionist model that was presented. The women's descriptions of violent incidents are presented when they (*a*) are the same incidents that the men describe when they discuss the notion of control, and (*b*) add additional information concerning the men's notion of control. Those instances where the notion of control was not discussed by the males are omitted from the analysis (see Appendix 10 for an example).

It is unclear why the batterers discussed control in some incidents and not in others. An examination of the data revealed that it was not consistently associated with other possible relevant factors. For example, it was not related to any specific contextual cue or cues that set the violence in motion. It was not associated with whether or not the incident had occurred recently or a long time ago. Finally, the batterers were no more likely to discuss incidents in terms of control in later as opposed to earlier interviews.

All but one man discussed at least one violent incident in detail in terms of control. Ronald described an incident with Kathy in terms of control only once. In order to understand why this is the case, it is important to examine whether there was anything unique about Ronald's and Kathy's relationship compared to the others in the sample. One difference is that after my first interview with Ronald and Kathy, they completely severed the relationship and were no longer in contact with each other. For those couples I interviewed over time (including Fred and Ann, even though Fred agreed to only two interviews with me), the partners continued communicating with each other and tried to work out the problems in the relationship in an effort to stay together. Some were successful and some were not. Those couples who were not successful still maintained some contact with each other up until my last interview with them.

I must also point out that the time lapse between my first and second interviews with Ronald and Kathy was seven months.[2] Three or four months after their mutual decision to end the relationship, Kathy stayed at Ronald's house, though they had separate bedrooms. Kathy moved out three months prior to my second interview with each of them, and they had not talked to each other since she left. It is possible that control no longer

---

[2]The large gap between my initial and second interviews with Ronald and Kathy was due to problems in gathering additional couples. Once I had obtained additional couples (approximately five months later) and interviewed them, I then arranged further interviews with all the respondents. This meant that the length of time between my initial interview and first follow-up with Ronald and Kathy was much longer than it was for any of the other couples.

becomes an issue for a batterer when the relationship ends and communication no longer exists.

Though Ronald did not describe any incidents with Kathy in terms of control, in our third interview he discussed a violent incident with a male friend that occurred the month prior. Ronald implied the notion of control in his description. Appendix 11 discusses this incident to illustrate how the model can be applied not only to abuse against women but also to violence toward men.

Evidence of the Symbolic Interactionist Model From the Findings

In each of the sections below, evidence for the interactionist model is presented. In all cases, the actual data is far more extensive than can be presented here. As mentioned in Chapter 5, the interactionist model highlights how the expectations of the "Me" about the self (to be violent or nonviolent) in the perception stage influence whether one carries out, checks, or inhibits the impulse to aggress in the manipulation stage. It is more likely that when the expectations of the "Me" are to be violent, the batterer will carry out the impulse to aggress rather than check or inhibit the impulse. When the expectations of the "Me" are to be nonviolent, it is more likely that the batterer will check or inhibit the impulse to aggress rather than carry out the impulse.

When presenting evidence for the model, I first note the contextual cue that influenced the batterer's response in the particular incident described. Second, and more importantly, I illustrate the various paths (A through F in Figure 5.1) that can exist in the violent act.

One thing that cannot be captured by the data is the nature of consummation. As discussed earlier, I did not ask the batterers how they felt immediately after an incident. If they focused on feeling guilty, then this would provide evidence for carrying out the impulse to aggress. If they focused on how their behavior was controlled, then this would provide evidence for checking the impulse to aggress. Instead, I asked about the behavioral reactions of each partner immediately following the incident. There is some suggestive evidence of the nature of consummation, and where this exists, I will note it. However, future research needs to examine more directly this feature of the model.

THE RELATIONSHIP BETWEEN THE EXPECTATIONS OF THE "ME" TO BE NONVIOLENT AND INHIBITING THE IMPULSE TO BE VIOLENT (Path A in Figure 5.1)

Larry and Kevin provide evidence that when the expectations of the "Me" are to be nonviolent, aggression may be inhibited. First, let me turn to Larry. Larry never experienced or witnessed violence when he was young.

Hence, he had a "Me" that was nonviolent. In our second interview, Larry described a disagreement he and Terri had regarding how to monitor an air-conditioning unit. Larry had become angry and wanted to hit her:

And rather than hit her, and that was my reaction, and that's my reaction right now as I think about it. I had my guard down. . . . I said, "I'm leaving.". . . And I left, and I drove around a couple of blocks.

Terri also told me about the argument they had over to monitor the air-conditioning unit. She did indicate that the argument ended with Larry leaving the house. Rather than acting on his impulse to aggress, Larry inhibited the impulse by leaving the situation, thus illustrating Path A in Figure 5.1.

Kevin provides another instance of inhibiting the impulse to aggress. Kevin came from a rather violent background. When he was young, both his parents beat him on several occasions. In addition, his dad encouraged him to have fist fights with his older sister.

Kevin and Lisa had been married for about 14 years. They both indicated that domestic violence began soon after they married and continued until I first met them. The majority of the violence occurred over finances. Soon after my initial meeting with each of them, they entered marriage counseling. It was during the counseling sessions that Kevin realized that his violence was inappropriate. He was learning alternative nonviolent ways to respond to Lisa. Therefore, the expectations of Kevin's "Me" changed, over time, from being violent to nonviolent. In our third interview, Kevin mentioned a recent argument that had occurred over their disconnected phone. Each was claiming that the other should have paid the phone bill. Kevin describes how he responded:

I remember because I got upset, and I walked into Lisa, and I said, I remember telling her, I said, "*I feel like I'm losing control.*" I said, "Right at that point." And she said, "Well, go outside and go for a walk. Just get out of the house." *So I just went outside, and I walked about six blocks, and I came back in, and I was fine.* [Emphasis added.]

Lisa discussed this incident in a similar way:

Recently we had an incident. . . The phone went dead. . . I thought, my gosh, they've cut the phone off. And so everybody was getting upset. . . he was getting really upset because I didn't pay the phone bill. . . But he said, "*Lisa, I'm losing control.*" He said, "*Why can't you just reach out to me and help me get control of the situation?*" I said, "Kevin, I've got my own problems right now." And he said, "But I really feel like I'm getting violent." I said, "Then leave. Just leave." . . . And he did. . . He did, and he went and walked around the block. [Emphasis added.]

Kevin turned to Lisa and told that he felt like he was "losing control." Taking Lisa's advice, Kevin left the situation, thereby sidestepping his impulse to aggress. Again, Path A in Figure 5.1 is revealed.

THE RELATIONSHIP BETWEEN THE EXPECTATIONS OF THE "ME" TO BE VIOLENT AND INHIBITING THE IMPULSE TO BE VIOLENT (Path *B* in Figure 5.1)

As mentioned in Chapter 5, when the expectations of the "Me" were to be violent, sometimes aggression was inhibited. My first interview with Frank will show that while this appeared to occur at first glance, upon closer inspection something else was actually taking place.

Frank indicated that when he was young, he often saw his father hit his mother. When Frank married, he was abusive to his wife, Ann. After he divorced and began dating Nancy, he turned his violence onto her. We can assume Frank had a violent "Me" as a result of prior socialization. However, in our first interview, Frank described a recent event that could have developed into a violent incident had he not controlled himself. As he says:

> We had an argument last night and the night before, and it got to the point where *I was going to strike her Saturday, but I didn't. I controlled it.* She thought I was. She said I had that look in my eye, and she was terrified to death that I was going to strike her. . . . *I could have just went off completely.* [Emphasis added.]

The Saturday incident that Frank mentioned occurred on the afternoon that Nancy and her children planned to go to a balloon race. Prior to leaving, Frank discovered that Nancy had her daughter buy her a pack of cigarettes from the market down the street. When Frank found out, he became upset and reminded Nancy that he had explicitly told her not to buy cigarettes because they could not afford them and that she had agreed. Now, he felt that she was going back on her word. The following happened as explained by Frank in our first interview:

> Well, I got pissed and I said, "We're not going." Really, I didn't have not one dollar. Not one dollar at all. And we were going to go to the balloon race. And I said, "Here I am and we're out of gas" but she's going to have to give me money to buy gas or whatever else we need to pay, she's going to have to foot the bill. And I said, "I don't have a dollar" and I said, "You just sent her to go get a pack of cigarettes." And I said, "I need gas right now and I need money for work next week. Can you give me money for work next week?" She said, "No." I said, "Now why did you go buy a pack of cigarettes?" I said, "You know how I feel about that issue. First of all you lied to me, told me she went to a neighbor's." I said, "Then you sent her to the store, and you knew." So she says, "Dammit, you're not going to control me." So everything got heated. So she looked at me, well she said, "I'm not going back in the house." I said, "Yeah you are, you're going to talk to me." She said, "I'm leaving." She was afraid I was going to jump on her. And, I felt that I was, I really did. I went in the house, and I said, "No. I'm not." I said, "All I want to do is talk to you."

Frank indicates that they finally talked things over and settled the issue. He notes that while he felt like he "was going to jump on her," he inhibited the impulse to aggress.

However, from Nancy's account of he same incident, it appears that she was the one who stopped Frank from hitting her and that Frank did not inhibit the violence himself. As she said in our first interview:

And the other night, when we started to go see the balloon race, but he started to go off on me then. He told me that I could never smoke another cigarette. And I just planned on moving out in August. And I told my mom, I said, "Sure, I won't smoke in front of him until August." Because I have no feelings for the man. I'm leaving. And, so, I bought a pack of cigarettes and we were getting ready to go to the balloon race, and he said something about me buying cigarettes, and I said, "Yeah, I bought a pack." And he goes, "Get out of the car." And he left my kids. We were supposed to take the kids to see a ballon race. They were all there. Got out of his car, walked to the house. And I thought, well, I'm not going in the house. And I set out in the grass with my kids, and he is going, "Just get in this house." And he said, "I said get in this house, now." He told me to get in the house and I said, "No." We sat down, and he said, "Why did you lie to me?" And I said, "Because I'm not going to give up my cigarettes." And I said, "I don't do anything. I can't go anywhere." I said, "I don't have much. Just let me smoke till I'm ready to stop." And he got really mad, and he walked into the house, and he come back out, and I started walking, my girlfriend works right at the restaurant right down the street. And he come running up behind me, and he grabbed me, and I turned around and looked at him like, "You're going to do something out here?" And he goes, "I need to talk to you. Come in the house and talk to me." And I knew he wanted to get me in the house really bad. And I said, "No." I said, "The police are on their way, Wimpy." I said, "You sit right here on this grass and talk to me where they can see us when they drive by." And he sat down and he said, "I need you." And I said, "If you need me, then you wouldn't be so damn violent toward me." I said, "You don't need me." I said, "What you want to do right now is hit me because I bought a pack of cigarettes after dad said no." And that's what he acts like, he's my dad. I said, "I'm not going to let you hit me again." And he said, "Just come in the house and talk to me." I said, "No." And he threw his arms again, and he walked back to the house. Okay? Oh, when he was running up toward me, Holly, my little girl just started screaming, she said, "Here he comes, Mommy." And she ran off and called the police. That's how I thought the police were coming. And so I was up to the restaurant, I was walking with my kids, and he pulled up and he goes, "Nancy, give me two dollars for gas, please." And I know the man had his money. I looked at him. And he goes, "Please, just two dollars for gas." I said, "Okay." So, when I handed him the money I knew he was going to try and grab my hand so I did it quick. And he did, he tried to grab my hand and pull me in the car. And I said, "I'm not getting in this car with you, Wimpy." And I said, "If I have to make a scene to protect myself, I will." And he said, "Just get in and go for a ride with me." And I said, "No." And he told me like five times, "Get in and go for a ride with me." And I said, "No." The park was right across the street. I said, "You go park your car over there and we'll sit in the park in front of people and talk. In the public eye." So he did that. And we sat and talked for two hours. And I said, "I know you were going to hurt me. I know you would have if I went into the house."

"No, I wouldn't have. I wasn't going to hit you, I just wanted to talk." I said, "No, you were going to hit me. You can't convince me different." And he goes, "Okay. Maybe."

From Nancy's scenario, she was aware of Frank trying to get her in an enclosed area, out of the public eye, so that he could have the opportunity to be violent towards her. Nancy's behavior directly influenced Frank's response of nonviolence. Therefore, the influence of Frank's violent "Me" was overriden by Nancy's actions.[3] That is, Frank was not aggressive to her not because he consciously inhibited the impulse, but because it was Nancy who refused to allow him the opportunity to be violent.

The Relationship Between the Expectations of the "Me" to be Violent and Checking the Impulse to be Violent (Path C in Figure 5.1)

Bill provides evidence that although the expectations of the "Me" are to be violent, the impulse to be violent may be controlled. Bill was very violent when he was young. He indicated that he learned from family and friends that violence was an appropriate response to conflict. Therefore, being violent partly defined his self-concept. Early in his youth, several assault and battery charges were brought against him. On two different occasions, he beat up his first girlfriend and the man she was then dating. On the second occasion, he was convicted of a felony and sent to prison for several years. Bill repeatedly beat up women he later dated. But, as already noted, he was violent to men as well. Furthermore, on one occasion, he and a friend beat up an elderly man and nearly killed him.

There was one point in his current relationship where he wanted to hit his partner but instead grabbed her and pushed her in a chair. The incident occurred around the time Bill was moving out of Jane's (his partner's) place. Bill had moved in with Jane in August 1985. They began to argue soon after he moved in, and a week after he moved in, he moved out. Bill did not identify a specific issue that prompted their arguments during that week other than that they "didn't get along." It was clear throughout their relationship, however, that Bill was jealous of other men Jane dated, and this initiated many arguments. It was clear from Bill's accounts that Jane did not want him around any longer because she wanted to date other men. He described the following incident in our third interview:

---

[3] One might argue that rather than Nancy's behavior overriding the influence of Frank's violent "Me," a different, nonviolent "Me" is being called up—a "Me" that expects one to be nonviolent in public. Given the data, there is no way of knowing whether a nonviolent "Me" now guides the situation.

The day I was going to leave, *I almost hit her.* . . . I told her, I said, "Yeah and where's my tapes that I left over here?" And she says, "There they is right there in the box." So I was getting ready to get my tapes, and she said, "Just move out of the way. I'll get them." So I stepped aside, and I guess I didn't step aside good enough for her. And she like pushed me. I already was pissed. . . . So I don't know how to act. And I started feeling strange. *The old ways started falling back in.* And I started to feel like I was being played for a sucker. And I really didn't like it. So when she pushed me out of the way, I said, "Jane," I said, "as long as you got a mouth to talk and you can say excuse me." She didn't say nothing, and she pushed me again. I grabbed her, and I just looked at her, and I just pushed her in this chair. And I did like this [clap of hands] here and she started doing this shit like I was going to hit her or something? And I said, "It ain't even worth it to put my hands on you." I said, "Now you going to act like the same damn fool. It don't make no difference how I act. You're going to use anything you can. [Emphasis added.]

Bill responded violently to the extent that he grabbed Jane and pushed her in the chair. He indirectly mentions the notion of control, however, and suggests that the violence was controlled because he was "almost" going to hit her, thus illustrating Path *C*. Perhaps one of the reasons Bill proceeded with some control was that he was participating in a male batterers group in which he was being taught the inappropriateness of using violence. Therefore, his "Me" was probably changing. This is supported by the fact that he mentions that "the old ways started falling back in." He wanted to hit her as he had hit women he had dated in the past. However, a "new Me," different from the "old Me," guided his behavior.

THE RELATIONSHIP BETWEEN THE EXPECTATIONS OF THE "ME" TO BE NONVIOLENT AND CHECKING THE IMPULSE TO BE VIOLENT (Path *D* in Figure 5.1)

Another path in the data was the expectations of the "Me" to be nonviolent and checking the impulse to aggress. Fred, Larry, and Doug provide evidence for this path. Let me first turn to Fred.

Fred indicated that he never experienced or witnessed violence when he was young. Moreover, he had never been violent to a woman prior to being violent to his wife, Ann. Fred indicated in our first interview that he was violent to Ann only once. Regarding that incident, he said the following:

It was the time when she stepped on my head, and I was laying there watching TV. And I hit her in the leg, and that's when I really hit her. . . . And when I went up to the employee counseling service and I got to talking to quite a few people, and I brought that question up, what would they do. Most everybody I asked said that that's probably what they would have done, too. And one friend said he'd probably slap their head off. *Which I hit her in the leg, and I never hit her in the face.* [Emphasis added.]

Though Fred had indicated that this was the only violent incident that had occurred, it should be pointed out that Ann recounted many other incidents. When I asked Fred why the incident had occurred, he said it was because he was not paying any attention to her. He claimed that Ann was a "spoiled brat" and that when she did not get her way, as when he was not paying attention to her, she would get angry. It appears that Fred is blaming Ann for his violence because she used violence first. Still, what precipitated this event remains unclear. Ann did not mention this episode as ever happening and so does not provide additional information on which to draw.

Fred's statement that he "hit her in the leg and not in the face" appears to illustrate Path D in Figure 5.1; that is, he controlled his violence because, in his view, hitting her in the face was a more uncontrolled reaction. However, alternative explanations may be offered for why Fred hit Ann in the leg and not the face. For example, because Ann stepped on Fred's head, her leg was closer to him than her face, and he could have hit her there because it was closer. Also, given that Fred makes this statement in the context of how other fellow employees said they would respond, he may be trying to neutralize the label of being a bad person. He may want to point out that other men could have enacted more severe violence (for example, hitting her in the face), and therefore he is not such a bad individual. Even if the latter interpretation is true, Fred may still be stating that his violence was controlled. It is unclear whether the neutralization of a negative label is an intended or unintended consequence of his statement regarding being in control.

As indicated earlier, Larry never experienced or witnessed violence when he was young. In addition, he had never beeen violent to women before Terri. In our first interview, he discussed an incident where he checked the impulse to aggress. The following incident occurred during an argument that Larry and Terri had over the fact that Larry had not brought their camping stove into the house after it had been outside for more than a week and, as Terri claimed, was getting rusty. Larry said that Terri was always "neurotically clean," and she wanted Larry to be that way as well. Larry felt that she was pushing him to change, and he did not want to change until he felt that he should and was ready. To a certain extent, therefore, Larry felt that Terri was trying to control his behavior. From Larry's description, the argument over the camping stove led to the following:

But I was in rage. This was just bullshit. It was hurtful bullshit, and it wasn't true. And I grabbed her, and the car was over here, and I grabbed, and I moved her about six feet up against the car and got in her face, and I think I was probably like this. And she made a couple threats like you'd better stop or I'm going to kick you or something like that, and it's like, she's not very big. The delivery sucked, as she says. But what the words were that I was saying was I was making points about that I have been doing fifty percent of my work, and here's what I've been doing. But I was just screaming at her. And again, I hate to say it, it's real hard to say it, but *that was restrained. I just would have as soon smashed her face.* That's what it felt like. What it felt like was you're hurting me so much, I can't stand this hurt, and *I want to just destroy you* so you won't hurt me any more. That's what it felt like. Which is a terrible solution, but it is not a solution. But that's what it felt like. I cannot handle this hurt. And then, like I pushed her, and she claims I've tried push her down. I don't really remember. I pushed her, again, away from the car. On the driveway. She didn't fall down. [Emphasis added.]

Larry indicates that his behavior was restrained, that he would have just as soon "smashed her face" and "destroyed her." He claims that instead, he grabbed her, "got in her face," and pushed her. Given that Larry came from a nonviolent background and that he controlled his violence during this incident, this excerpt illustrates Path *D* in Figure 5.1.

THE RELATIONSHIP BETWEEN THE EXPECTATIONS OF THE "ME" TO BE VIOLENT AND CARRYING OUT THE IMPULSE TO BE VIOLENT (Path *E* in Figure 5.1)

As mentioned in Chapter 5, it was more likely that the batterers carried out the impulse to aggress when the expectations of the "Me" were to be violent. This is illustrated in Henry and Jackie's relationship. Henry never saw his father hit his mother. Furthermore, he claimed that he had never hit a woman before his current partner, Jackie. Therefore, the expectations of Henry's "Me" were to be nonviolent.

However, what seemed to occur over time with Henry, especially beginning with the second incident, is that the expectations of his "Me" changed to being violent toward women. This change appeared to have been influenced by Jackie's use of violence, which she first used in their second incident and which Henry claims influenced him to use violence as well. As he says:

I felt, hitting a woman? That had never occurred to me as a possible way to resolve. She started that by coming up and hitting me as a way of resolving it. I decided I would get engaged in that kind of conduct, too. It seemed she validated it by doing it to me.

This illustrates the interactive and developmental nature of the "Me" in violence. Because the expectations of the "Me" entail how others expect you to behave, it is possible that Henry's "Me" changed because he thought that Jackie expected him to behave violently or that it was an acceptable form of behavior, as is revealed in Jackie's description of their second violent incident:

I walked in, and I threw these flowers that he had given me the week before. I threw them on the floor. And I ripped up this picture he had of me. And I was really ready to fight. I was just furious. And we did. I slapped him. I'm sure he told you about this incident. I sat on him, and I slapped him, and I said, *"No guy has ever let me get away with slapping them."* And I slapped him, like, oh, I'd say three or four times, and I said, *"Why don't you hit me back?"* And again, I think I was trying to sabotage it. Well, he didn't just slap me back, he slugged me hard, real hard across the mouth. I had a big, big bruise. He just went like this. And he hit me so hard that I flew off the bed and stuff. [Emphasis added.]

Jackie's remarks of "No guy has ever let me get away with slapping them" and "Why don't you hit me back?" indicates that she expected Henry to respond violently, and when he initially did not, she made remarks encouraging him to do so. Henry apparently recognized that Jackie's expectations were for him to respond violently, and he inevitably fulfilled those expectations. This explanation is not meant to blame Jackie for Henry's violence but rather is to suggest how the expectations of other's (defining the "Me") in the interactive setting relate to violent conduct.

The excerpts above highlight the idea that respondents understand violence as an interactional production. Jackie's words and behaviors are very much a part of Henry's understanding of his production of violence. Violence cannot be understood in isolation of the women's actions and reactions, and this must be accounted for in any theoretical understanding of domestic violence (Denzin, 1984b).

Prior to their second violent incident, Henry had taken a summer job in Chicago. Jackie would visit him almost every weekend, but she claimed that the visits were not enjoyable because they would often end up arguing. She felt that he was unhappy with his job and was taking it out on her. At one point during the summer, Jackie discovered that Henry had gone out with another women whom Jackie happened to know. Though Henry had told her that it was just a business dinner, Jackie was still upset and jealous about it. As suggested in Chapter 5, cross-sex friendships often caused jealousy on one partner's or both partner's part. Jackie felt that Henry had been treating her badly all summer and then turned around and wined and dined a woman whom Jackie thought was elitist and cared only about money. She ended up traveling to see Henry to tell him how upset and angry she was about his date. On her way to see him, she began drinking.[4] Henry indicated that when she arrived, the following occurred:

So, she came up to my apartment in Chicago and didn't talk to me but proceeded to berate me for about two hours, and then she finally hit me in the face and in the stomach. And, I was upset. *I'm laying on my bed and finally reached over to her and with the back of my hand just slapped her.* She got a black lip from it and cried and

---

[4] Both Henry and Jackie admitted that violence generally occurred when they had been drinking. However, they typically drank when they were together, and violence did not always occur. Therefore, alcohol use was associated with violence but did not cause it. Henry indicated that their drinking made the violence worse, while Jackie said it hurried the violence along or made it easier for violence to erupt. Research has shown that alcohol consumption decreases self-monitoring (Hull, 1981). In this way, it may be less likely that the "Me" interrupts the actions of the "I" and thus that violence associated with drinking is less subject to control through self-monitoring.

was all hurt. That black lip went away, and then we went on vacation. We had decided a few weeks later that things would be okay. *I wouldn't hit her, and it was ugly, and I'm sorry and this and this.* [Emphasis added.]

Jackie described the incident in this way:

Well, he didn't just slap me back, he slugged me hard, real hard across the mouth. I had a big, big bruise . . . And he hit me so hard that I flew off the bed.

During this incident, Henry admits to slapping Jackie although Jackie indicates that he "slugged" her. It is assumed that he carried out the impulse to aggress. This illustrates Path *E* in Figure 5.1. Furthermore, Henry's remark of "I'm sorry" illustrates the guilt associated with postconsummation upon carrying out the impulse to aggress.

THE RELATIONSHIP BETWEEN THE EXPECTATIONS OF THE "ME" TO BE NONVIOLENT AND CARRYING OUT THE IMPULSE TO BE VIOLENT (Path *F* in Figure 5.1)

Ronald provides evidence where, though the expectations of the "Me" are to be nonviolent, the impulse to be violent is still carried out. Ronald's past relationships with women were generally nonviolent. Prior to his relationship with Kathy, he admitted to hitting only one woman. To a large degree, therefore, the use of violence towards women was foreign to Ronald. As the relationship between Ronald and Kathy developed, Ronald began to be violent. In the incident cited below, Kathy was telling Ronald about another man she was seeing. Ronald responded in the following way:

We were sitting on the floor facing each other, and I kicked her in the chest real hard and knocked her down, and then I got on top of her and started slamming her on the floor, and she said her head started to hurt real bad. She said she had a headache for three days.

Kathy verifies the occurrence of this incident:

I was talking about Philip which is the man I moved in with for a while . . . that was the time when I think he kicked me in the chest, and I think he came over and held my shoulders and slammed my head against the floor. And that was the time he actually hurt me . . . like my jaw was sore.

From this incident, it appears that Ronald carried out the impulse to aggress, thus illustrating Path *F* in Figure 5.1.

THE INTERACTIVE COMPONENT OF THE MODEL

Having provided illustrations regarding the various paths in the model, one thing is clear. The woman does affect the expectations and behavior of the man. Though she does not determine the path that the man's behavior will take, she does influence it. In the case of Henry and Jackie, it was shown that Jackie's expectations of Henry's behavior affected Henry's definition of his "Me," and eventually his behavior.

A woman's behavior can inhibit violence on the part of the man. This was revealed in the incident between Frank and Nancy discussed above. Frank indicated that he inhibited the impulse to aggress; from Nancy's account, however, she remained in a public area so that he would not hit her. Hence, Nancy's behavior affected the particular path of behavior that Frank enacted in that situation.

In addition, when interpreting a situation, it is important to incorporate both the man's and woman's perspective. The following incident between Doug and Wendy illustrates this point. Doug and Wendy provide different descriptions of what happened during their last violent episode. Before presenting their different descriptions, I will highlight the history of Doug's violence. Though Doug never saw his father hit his mother, he sometimes hit his sister and, later, women he dated. Doug admitted to being very violent toward his ex-wife, including raping her. Several months after dating Wendy, Doug started to use violence on her.

Doug described, in detail, what happened in their last violent episode. I will concentrate on the early part of this episode in order to illustrate how Doug claimed to have checked the impulse to aggress by proceeding to be violent but with control. Then, I will discuss the later part of this incident in order to show how Doug implied that his control eventually broke down and he carried out the impulse to aggress.

Both Doug and Wendy indicated that their last violent episode was caused by Doug's refusal to buy toilet paper for the house.[5] On the Saturday morning of the incident, Wendy came into the bedroom and asked Doug if he had bought the toilet paper. He said he had not. In our third interview, Doug recounted the first part of the violent episode in this way:

She pulled the pillow away from me. Started pounding it, hitting me with it. And I was stark naked. . . . *And I picked her up by her arms and carried her down the hallway and set her in the baby's room and held onto to her near the crib*, and I said, "Hey," I says, "we've got a baby here. We don't need to be fighting in front of this baby." And I was reprimanding her for coming in and screaming at me especially. *And I took her up and carried her out of there and took her into the living room, and I sat her down on the couch* and I said, "Now, we're going to call John, and you're going to ask him for some toilet paper." Ha. Not me. I was just trying to inject some humor there. . . . Well, I thought I was doing real good because *I was just like restraining her* and got her to the telephone. And was going to call John. *And I thought, "Well, that's a lot better than just knocking the shit out of her."* [Emphasis added.]

---

[5]This precipitating factor will be discussed in greater detail in the discussion section.

Doug claims that he behaved in a very controlled fashion by taking hold of her and eventually getting her into the living room to call John (his male battering group counselor) so that they could get some help to resolve the conflict and prevent the violence. Men in the batterers group were told to call John if they felt the urge to be violent. Doug felt that he was exhibiting controlled behavior as opposed to "knocking the shit out of her." Therefore, Doug's initial response to Wendy's violence was controlled.

However, the entire episode did not end with a call to John; he later carried out the impulse to aggress. As Doug said in our third interview:

In my top pocket, I had his phone number and stuff in my shirt. My shirt was in the living room still. And I took it out of there, and she said, "What's the number?" and she started dialing, and she dialed the first 555, and I started reading out the other numbers to her and she said something smart to me, and that's the straw that breaks the camel's back. [What did she say?] I don't even know. I have no idea. It was her tone of voice and all kinds of stuff that set me off. Just the fact that she wouldn't call him and get some help, and she wanted to continue arguing. I had no idea what she said. I cannot remember. And I don't even care. It probably doesn't matter. And I backhanded her. Like that. It was one stroke but it kind of got a hold of her at the time when I hit her. And my ring caught her, and she was bleeding above her eye. Had like a cut there between her eyes. . . . And, it wasn't my intention to hit her. My intention was to get her out of my space and to have her leave me alone and to get a hold of John and have him calm us down or something. *But I didn't intend to hit her. I thought I was taking great measures to not hit her. And she was taking great measures to get hit. And she got hit. To me, it was a knee jerk response to her last remark.* [Emphasis added.]

Doug views his response as out of control by the mere fact that he identifies it as automatic, that is, a "knee jerk response." Doug implies that his control breaks down early in the episode and is no longer effective in sidestepping the impulse to aggress.

Wendy's description of what happened provides a different interpretation of Doug's behavior. She said in our third interview:

And I grabbed one of my pillows off the bed, and I tossed it at him. And I missed him. And he jumped up out of the bed and grabs my arm around behind my back, and he like pushes me down the hallway and into the baby's room, and he holds me over a crib. I've got like my hand on the wall so I don't fall on her bed, and he's still got my arm behind me, and he started hitting me. [What did he do?] First of all, he like backhanded me and caught this side of my face, and it was all bruised. And he hit me again like on this side, and he caught me down and under here, and this eye was all black and blue. It had almost swollen shut. And we got into the living room somehow, and he picked the phone up off the end table, and he tossed it at me, and he says, "Call John." And I said, "What do you want me to tell John?" And he came up at me with his fist, and he hit me like right here, and he cut my forehead open and cut my eye wide open.

Wendy's story suggests that Doug did not control his violence early on. Instead, it appears that Doug carried out the impulse to aggress from the moment she threw the pillow at him.[6] This not only illustrates how opposing viewpoints may result when both partner's accounts are considered, but it also calls into question whether or not Doug's violent was controlled in the early part of this episode.

Doug could be claiming that he had control during the early part of the episode in order to neutralize the label of being a bad person. By suggesting that he made attempts to deter the violence, he may be implying that it was not his fault that the episode resulted in violence. In our third and fourth interviews, he repeatedly indicated that Wendy "provoked" the violence, which supports the interpretation that he is not to be blamed. It would be interesting to learn how Doug would have explained Wendy's black and blue eyes. Wendy claims he bruised her eyes when they were in their child's bedroom. Doug's description makes no claim to having done this. Given the different scenarios by each partner, one still cannot discount the possibility that Doug perceived his behavior as more controlled early on despite the actual violence that resulted. Perhaps the violence would have been worse had he not been controlling it to the extent the felt he had.

In the incident between Doug and Wendy, Doug indicated that he first controlled the impulse to aggress and then carried out the impulse. However, Wendy's account opens up the possibility that control operated quite differently from what Doug claimed, as when she indicated that he carried out the impulse to aggress from the moment the incident began. It should be pointed out that both Doug's and Wendy's descriptions are accounted for in Figure 5.1. While Doug's description implies that early on he took Path *C* and only later took Path *E*, Wendy's description connotes Doug took Path *E* from the moment the violence erupted.

In sum, the actions, reactions, and interpretations of the woman cannot be ignored when attempting to understand domestic violence. Additionally, though the woman's *behavior* is not explicitly incorporated into the diagram, it is assumed to be an important feature in the model of the violent act. Figure 5.1 should not be interpreted as describing only the man's behavior, for example. His behavior does not exist in a vacuum and can be understood only in relation to how the woman behaves.

A DISCUSSION OF THE CONTEXTUAL CUES

I identified the particular contextual cues that influenced the detailed violent incidents presented in this chapter. The majority of the cues had the underlying theme of control. In some cases, this control was explicit. For

---

[6]Wendy noted in our fourth interview that she later went to the doctor and discovered that Doug had cracked two of her ribs during the early part of this violent incident.

example, Frank and Nancy had an argument over the fact that Frank told Nancy not to buy cigarettes, and Nancy bought them anyway. In other cases, the control was more implicit. For example, Larry and Terri argued over how to monitor an air-conditioning unit. Larry felt that it should have been monitored one way, while Terri thought it should be monitored another way. As Terri said in our second interview:

[Would the topics be different? What would bring you to the point in one direction as opposed to the other?] Yeah. I think, they were almost exclusively some kind of control issue about the way we were going to do something. . . . And often, I think we're finding . . . that [it's] almost exclusively something that I have said or that he says is misread. I'd say something, and he assumes that I mean, dammit this is the way we're going to do it. When I might say, "Why don't we paint the bookshelf blue." And what I mean is, "What do you think about blue?" And how he takes that is, "She's trying to tell me that we have to paint the bookcase blue." Okay? And I would do the same thing. So, I think almost exclusively, those are the kinds of things we fight about.

Terri indicates that how she says something and what she really means by it may be two different things. In the meantime, Larry believes that she is saying what is to be done when she sees it as just a suggestion. Terri claimed that she often misinterpreted what Larry said as well. In fact, later in this interview, she directly discusses the argument over monitoring the air-conditioning unit as an example of how she misread what Larry was saying, and took his suggestion in a defensive way:

This Sunday, Larry was over, and we ended up in an argument over the thermostat. Larry said, "I turned the air-conditioner on automatic so that it would get colder in here." And I said, "No. That doesn't work. You have to leave the fan on. You have to leave it on fan because when it's on automatic, the fan shuts off." And he immediately got real angry. And I don't remember what he said from that point, but then immediately, we were both yelling at each other. And I was saying, "No. You have to leave it on fan because if you leave it on fan, then the air is always circulating." And he said, "Well, when I had a thermostat like that, we left it on automatic, and it always worked fine. It's obviously too hot in here." And we both went back and forth. So we talked about that just yesterday in the counseling session, what was going on. And, for me, I had spent some time carefully figuring out what it would do; carefully figuring out how to work the thermostat control. And so when he said, "I turn it on automatic" I felt like he was discounting all the work that I had put into figuring out how to do it and was telling me that I didn't know how to work the thermostat. And he thought the exact same thing, that I was telling him that he didn't know how to work the thermostat, that we were both right and that neither one of us would budge. He didn't know that I had spent time to figure out how the thermostat works, and I didn't know that he was just making a suggestion that we try it on automatic to see what would happen, see if it made a difference.

The fact that neither one of them would "budge" indicates that each wanted the power to determine how the unit should be operated. It was not until they discussed it in counseling that Terri realized that she was misinterpreting Larry's remarks as a demand instead of a suggestion.

Therefore, close examination of the contextual cues influencing violent episodes suggests that, to a large extent, control is the underlying issue. Henry and Jackie typically fought over who the other person could go out with. Henry, more so than Jackie, felt that he had the right to tell her that she could not go out with other men, thus controlling who she could or could not see. Bill and Jane had similar problems. In fact, during my last interview with Bill, he claimed that the previous day he was on his way to Jane's house to kill her because he had seen her with another man, but he was picked up for reckless driving before he could get there.

Mike and Kay, Wendy and Doug, Kevin and Lisa, and Frank and Nancy all fought over finances. Control over money matters often led to violent incidents. In some cases, money was not the single issue involved, as in the case of Wendy and Doug, where it was embedded in other issues of control.

Wendy and Doug had a violent incident over the issue of toilet paper. As mentioned in Chapter 5, arguments over money matters often resulted in violence, but to interpret an argument over who was to buy the toilet paper as an example of an argument over finances may be carrying the issue too far. Let me explore the possibility that the issue was probably something else, that what precipitates a violent incident may be much more complex than what appears on the surface. Moreover, the issue of control, whether in the realm of finances or friendships, may operate on different levels.

Early in my third interview with Doug, just before he told me about the violent incident, he indicated that Wendy expected him to play the provider role. He noted that one of the roles as provider included the purchase of household items such as toilet paper. Because he did not believe he should have the responsibility of being the provider, however, he did not think he should have to buy the toilet paper. Throughout my interviews with Doug, here and elsewhere, he repeatedly noted that Wendy wanted to marry him but that he was not committd to her in that way. He did not feel any responsibility to her or his child (whom Wendy recently gave birth to) and did not intend to play the provider role.

In my third interview with Wendy, she indicated that in the week prior to the incident, tension had been building. Doug would often be out until five or six in the morning, and Wendy would not know where he was. This upset her. If he was home, he would have a friend over, and they would be up until three or four o'clock in the morning watching television and keeping Wendy awake. During this time, Wendy was preparing their child's christening. She was spending time cleaning the house and getting things in order for the event. On the Wednesday prior to the violence, she had asked Doug to buy some toilet paper because she did not have any money. She felt that this was the least Doug should do because she was working so hard getting ready for the christening. Doug refused. The morning of the

Saturday christening, she asked Doug if he had bought the toilet paper. She was concerned because her parents would be in town in a matter of hours and she needed toilet paper for the house.

It may be argued that the issue here is not finances, but rather a challenge to Doug to act responsibly in the relationship. Doug interpreted Wendy's request to buy toilet paper as an act indicative of being responsible in the relationship. Wendy might have interpreted it as taking care of a domestic chore for her and the baby. Because Doug did not want to assume responsibility, conflict arose.

However, the issue may be finances. Wendy may have thought that Doug should assume some of the burden in providing for her and the child. Up until this point, Wendy had taken care of all the finances in the family. Doug had been unemployed since he met her, so Wendy paid for the rent, food, and household items. Because Wendy did not have any money at the time, perhaps she felt that was the least Doug could do for her: he owed her that much. Further, an incident had occurred about a month earlier where an argument arose over finances. Though the incident was not very violent, it does indicate that this was not the first time conflict occurred over money.

To further complicate matters, Wendy and Doug appeared not to be communicating well. Doug was rarely home and if he was, he usually had a friend over. There was minimal communication between them. It could have been that this incident was a response to this lack of communication. It did provide the opportunity for them to eventually sit down and talk, after the incident, when each of them was more open to communication with the other.

Given the prior discussion, what are we to make of what precipitated the violence? Was it control over how much responsibility Doug was to assume in the relationship? Was it control over finances? Or was it a lack of prior communication? It is possible that all three elements could have been operating, and that none, by itself, adequately explains the cause of the violence. The important thing is that control may operate at different levels. What appears as the issue up front, getting the toilet paper, may be embedded in control over finances which, in turn, may be embedded in a larger issue: here, control over responsibility in the relationship.

Summary

Evidence from the data has been presented in order to illustrate the basis of the interactionist model that was presented in Chapter 4. The evidence has come from detailed discussions by the men of the notion of control. The women's descriptions have been included when they have provided additional relevant information concerning the men's feelings of being in or out of control when they were violent.

To reiterate, the interactionist model describes the relationship between violence and the notion of control. Particular contextual cues set the violence in motion. The batterer's initial, impulsive reaction is to respond aggressively. Given the expectations of the "Me" to be violent or nonviolent, the batterer may (*a*) inhibit his violent response, (*b*) use violence but with some control (checking the impulse to aggress), or (*c*) use violence with no control (carrying out the impulse to aggress) and either proceed as originally planned or proceed as originally planned but with increased violence. Guilt may be more likely to occur after carrying out the impulse to aggress, while a focus on the controlling aspects of the behavior may be more likely to occur after checking the impulse to aggress.

It is important to point out that because many of these men were in some sort of treatment, whether it was a male batterers group, couple or individual counseling program, the expectations of the "Me" were probably affected by such treatment. Therefore, changing from a violent to nonviolent individual was likely to be influenced by therapeutic help. This has important implications for therapy programs that want to help the batterer, for it suggests that changing the expectations of the "Me" can greatly influence behavioral changes.[7] This is not to say that one must be in treatment for expectations of nonviolence to exist. There are other ways that this can be accomplished, for example, by not receiving support from friends and family for violent behavior.

In the findings, I illustrated how the different expectations of the "Me" in the perception stage related to the various responses a batterer might make in the manipulation stage. As was shown, however, the relationship between the perception and manipulation stages is complex. A batterer who comes from a violent background may have learned that violence is a legitimate way to resolve conflict. Therefore, when a conflict situation arises with his partner, he may perceive that others expect him to be violent and thus will carry out the impulse to aggress without any regard for controlling it. However, returning to the findings on Bill, it was found that though he came from a violent background, he perceived that when some incidents occurred, his aggression was controlled. The perception of control may have been due to the fact that Bill was beginning to learn, through participation in a male batterers group, that violence against women was inappropriate. What this suggests is that in order to understand the relationship between the expectations of the "Me" and whether violence is controlled or not, we need to have a clear, rich, and detailed understanding (through in-depth discussions) of the batterers' past and present experiences. Only then can we make some sense out of why they behave (or think they behave) as they do.

It is interesting that Henry claims that the first time he hit Jackie, she had hit him first. It is possible that the woman's behavior does have some influence on whether or not the batterer is violent. Henry thought that Jackie

---

[7] This will be discussed in greater detail in Chapter 8.

legitimized his impulse to be violent because she used violence first. As mentioned before, he may have thought that she expected him to be violent to her, and he fulfilled those expectations. Therefore, when we talk about the expectations of the "Me," we need to consider what expectations the women may be signalling to the men.

Some violent incidents may have more than one act. How the act is defined determines whether or not an incident is made up of more than one act. I noted earlier that an act begins with a cue that sets in motion the impulse to respond. The act ends when it is perceived that the impulse has been carried out. In the incident between Ronald and his friend (Appendix 11), the act began when Ronald's friend started screaming at him and ended after Ronald kicked the flower pot and left. The incident did not end here, however. His friend's look initiated a second cue and thus a second act. Ronald returned and they talked; Ronald felt that the discussion could have led him to be violent again but that he inhibited the impulse to aggress. The act ended after they completed the conversation.

Some acts may not end and instead may be a cue for another act. For example, in the incident between Doug and Wendy, the first act was not completed simply because Wendy did not end up calling John. Instead, towards the end of this act, Doug claims Wendy said something (Wendy says it was "What should I tell him?") and that this made him angry enough to hit her. Therefore, Wendy's question at the end of the first act served as another cue, initiating a second act. This second act was completed to the extent that the impulse to aggress was carried out.

One final remark should be made regarding the findings. In Chapter 4, I discussed the fact that the men perceived their emotions as out of control when they were violent. The evidence in this chapter provides very little support for the fact that when describing specific violent incidents, the men indicate that their emotions are out of control. In my sample, the only batterer who does this is Mike. There may be two reasons why the men do not mention their emotions as out of control with regard to a specific incident. First, in our society, women more than men are encouraged to talk about their emotions. Second, I did not ask the batterers how they felt during a particular violent incident. The data reveals that when the men talk about their emotions as out of control, it is in a very general way, without reference to a specific violent incident. Future research may need to pursue how the men feel during an incident in order to capture the affective dimension of the violent act.

It is important to reiterate that domestic violence must be understood as a function of how the man *and* the woman behave. In other words, the man's violence does not occur in isolation from the woman's response. She influences the kind of "Me" he has and the particular path he takes. Future researchers must incorporate this feature into their understanding of violence in order to identify the nature and dynamics of violence.

7
Control as Object: An Analysis of Violence Over Time

Violence occurs at a given point in time and reoccurs over time. This chapter focuses on the nature of the violence over time and provides evidence that control again becomes a meaningful object. However, control takes on two different meanings when respondents describe the violence over time. First, repeated acts of violence are associated with attempts to control the woman. In this sense, the meaning of control may be understood as external in nature, in that the target of control is the woman and not the batterer himself. Second, for those couples who, over time, no longer experience repeated acts of violence, the man's behavior is described and understood in terms of how he now controls himself: that is, his emotions and behavior and how he avoids controlling his partner. In this way, the meaning of control is internal in nature, in that control involves the man changing past emotional and behavioral responses. Both of these meanings of control are evidenced in this chapter.

Two general phases characterize the violence over time. In the first phase, there is a general emergence of violent behavior. That this emergence exists is highlighted by the fact that most of the batterers had never been violent to a woman prior to their current relationship. Over time, not only does the violence become a feature of the relationship, but it also becomes more frequent and more severe. This first phase is directly related to the man wanting to control his partner. As will be discussed in greater detail later, early violent incidents may be carried out to satiate the impulse to aggress. Over time and through the process of learning, violence may be carried out in order to control the other.

In the second phase, there is a movement from violence to nonviolence as the men gain control over their aggressive behavior. About half of the couples were experiencing nonviolence in their relationship when I last met with them. This movement toward nonviolence was associated with the batterers reaching an awareness that their emotions and behavior were out of control when they were violent. Having realized this, they made attempts to control their anger and behavior in order to stop the violence. Moreover, a movement toward nonviolence was associated with the batterers' realization that they wanted to control their partner. This realization led to attempts to avoid controlling their partner.

This chapter, therefore, highlights how, over time, violence emerges in a relationship and takes the form of instrumental violence and then how that violence stops when the men control their emotions and behavior and avoid controlling their partner. As will be shown, control as object is intimately connected to this process. It is likely that had I not collected data on these couples over time, I would not have been able to capture this process. More research in domestic violence is certainly needed to examine violence over time.

Walker (1979b) was the first to examine the reoccurrence of violence. She indicated that there was a cycle of violence and that three stages characterized this cycle: tension building, the acute battering incident, and the loving stage. Once the loving stage ended, the violence would arise again through the emergence of tension building. Thus, there was a continual recycling of violence over time. There are some problems with Walker's research, however.

First, her cycle is based on one-shot interviews with abused women. Second, she does not identify the source of the tension building or acute battering incident. As indicated in Chapter 5, I found that when conflict over control, finances, or friendships appeared, there was a tendency for violence to result. Therefore, the issue of control seems to be an important feature in domestic violence.

Third, Walker's identification of the calm, loving stage is, in part, a direct result of the fact that she interviewed only women. In this study, the loving stage appeared primarily in the women's accounts. The majority of the women indicated that their mate would be apologetic and loving after a violent incident. Only Doug mentioned that a honeymoon stage existed. Henry mentioned that sometimes after a violent incident they would try to make up. Although Mike, Larry, Kevin, and Frank displayed guilt feelings over their violence towards their partner, they never clearly identified a loving stage.

Two interpretations can be made regarding the fact that the men, in general, do not mention a loving stage. On the one hand, the loving stage may exist only from the woman's perspective. Because her partner's behavior after an incident becomes very salient to her, she focuses all her attention on him, especially on how he will behave next. Any act of kindness that the man may show toward her after the violence may be interpreted as a display of how much her mate loves her. Perhaps the woman wantes to make this interpretation because she recently experienced violence, an indication that her partner did not love her. Thus, women experience a contrast effect. First, they experience their mate behaving violently and unlovingly towards them, and then they experience their partner being nonviolent and loving.

On the other hand, what happens after a violent incident may be understood from the man's perspective. The men may be affectionate, caring, or loving to their partner after an incident not because they want to express how they truly feel about their partner, but because they want to relieve themselves of guilt feelings they have for having been violent. In this sense, the third stage is not a loving stage so much as it is a forgiveness stage.

This research examines the longitudinal nature of violence, not in terms of the cycle of violence (which has its problems as mentioned above), but rather in terms of its relationship to control. First, I address the emergence of violent behavior and show how violence, over time, takes on an instrumental flavor. Then I examine the movement toward nonviolent behavior.

Phase One: The Emergence of Violence in Terms of Instrumentality

I argue that when a man is first violent, his violence is carried out in order to satiate the impulse to aggress. Therefore, early battering is indicative of wanting to strike back at another who has caused one psychological or physical injury. Over time and through learning, however, the violence takes on an instrumental flavor, that is, to control the woman. Hence, early battering has the long-term consequences of controlling the other's behavior.

The argument that later battering is characteristic of instrumental violence is based on suggestive evidence from the data. All but one man in this sample (Bill, discussed below) had been violent to his partner for at least four months prior to my initial interview with them. During interviews with the men over the four-month period, the instrumental nature of the violence was revealed at one point or another. This therefore suggests that instrumental violence does occur in later violence because the respondents had been involved in violent relationships for some time. In additon, when respondents reflected upon early incidents, they generally did not describe them in terms of wanting to control the women. This provides further evidence that instrumental violence is more likely to occur in later violence.

It is unclear how long it would take for the act to be transformed from impulsive to instrumental violence. The length of time necessary for this transformation cannot be addressed with the present data. First, I did not interview most couples immediately after their first violent incident, which would have provided a starting point in determining the change from impulsivity to instrumentality over time. With the exception of Bill's violence toward Jane, the violence for all the couples had begun at least four months prior to my initial meeting with them. All of the respondents mentioned the issue of controlling the woman in my first interview with them, which suggests that the transformation had occurred sometime between the first incident and my initial meeting with them.

The transformation does appears to exist, however, given my interviews with Bill. Bill entered the male battering program and agreed to participate in this research because he felt that he was getting closer to being violent towards Jane. He had a history of being violent to other women. This suggests that a person learns to be violent with each new partner. The first time Bill was violent to Jane was during the month following our initial interview. Prior to and immediately following this incident, our interviews focused on the fact that he felt out of control whenever he became angry at Jane, thus highlighting impulsivity. For example, he said this late in our second interview:

See cause she was supposed to have been jumped at least fifty times by me. If I wasn't trying to work on myself. I was trying to work with myself before I got into this program. Cause the way I got into the program, I said, *"I want to get into this program so it won't happen.* Cause I know one of these days it will." If it ever do, *I'd probably wind up with a murder charge. Cause it's still all pent up inside from what she's been doing. And it would probably just snap me.* It won't be nothing that can be corrected in a day or two. *It would probably just snap.* [Emphasis added.]

Although Bill indicates that, for the most part, he has controlled his behavioral reaction to Jane, he characterizes the possibility of violent behavior in the future as impulsive in nature, that is, one of these days he'll "just snap." Moreover, although the issue of control exists, Bill indicates that it is his own behavior he is controlling, not Jane's, by indicating that the battering program will help him from behaving impulsively.

It was not until our last interview that suggestive evidence begins to appear regarding Bill's need to control Jane through violence. On several occasions, Bill had seen Jane with her ex-husband. Every time Bill saw this, he got angry because he did not want her seeing her "ex." Jane felt that she had the right to see who she wanted. Bill finally got so angry one night regarding this issue that he went over to her house with the intention, he claimed, to kill her. However, on his way to her house, he was picked up by the police for reckless driving. The point, however, is that Bill saw the violence as a response to Jane not doing what he asked, that is, to stop seeing her "ex."

When tracing the impulsive to instrumental transformation of violence, it may not be enough to have a couple's first violent incident as a starting point. Other factors may need to be considered. For example, batterers who do not experience any punishment for behaving violently may perceive violence more readily as a mechanism for control than batterers who experience periodic punishment. Therefore, instrumental violence may take shape at a faster rate for the former than latter batterers.

As mentioned, the respondents indicated, upon reflection, how the violence assumed an instrumental quality. I will address the characterization of violence in terms of instrumentality in order to highlight the fact that later violence is often deliberate and carried out for the purpose of maintaining power and control over the woman. In order to understand the nature of instrumental violence, I identified three stages that helped describe the dynamics that are involved. These include (*a*) challenging the right to control, (*b*) losing control and using violence to regain control, and (*c*) regaining control through the other's submission. Let me begin by discussing the first stage of the instrumental act.

STAGE ONE: CHALLENGING THE RIGHT TO CONTROL

During our last interviews, Kevin and Lisa discussed how violence was primarily carried out in order to control Lisa. When I asked Kevin what it was that caused him to use or not use violence, he said:

It's kind of a two-edged sword, Jan. One, you want to leave, but by leaving, it's back to this giving ground concept. And there were times when I tried to leave and I'd start to leave, and Lisa would say one more thing instead of just not saying anything and let me get outside. She'd say something else, and it would be anything. It wouldn't have to be pertinent to what we were fighting about. Just the fact that she opened her mouth with that much anger would be what I viewed as one more stroke of the flip of anger or the breaking point. It was just the fact that she wouldn't keep quiet. She wouldn't shut up. She wouldn't let me go and discuss it when I cooled off. So it's a two-edged sword. One, the intensity of the personalities in there are so tight that being a person can just quit talking or quit yelling or quit saying anything and just turn it off. And the other is by leaving, you feel like you've given ground. And you won't let them leave. *I wouldn't let Lisa leave because, if she left, that was her telling me that I don't have to do what you say. And it's a matter of control. You want it your way. If I want to leave, I want to leave because I can leave. You can't leave because I told you to stay and be quiet. And the whole thing boils down to a matter of control.* Well, I had to overcome that. I had to just sit there, and I had to say, "I am going to leave. And no matter what you say, I am not going to turn back. I am going to leave, and I'm going for a walk." And I had to just force myself to do that. And I'd get outside, and there was almost an uncontrollable desire to return and get back into it. I just had to walk and think about it and just cool down. Let things lie. [Emphasis added.]

Lisa said this in our final interview:

[Now what you were really saying was that there's control sometimes but not necessarily violence but the cause of violence has always been control.] Mm. Hmm. Oh yeah, in fact, Kevin tried that tonight. Hah. Cause, as we were leaving, he goes, "Why are you upset?" I said, "I had a nasty conversation with Bank Americard." He goes, "Well stop, what is it?" And I said, "Kevin, I'm late. I've got to go." And I was walking, and he said, "Stop. Stop." And I said, "You want to talk to me, come over here and talk to me." He said, "No. Stop. Come back here and talk to me." And I said, "If you want to talk to me, come to the car and talk to me." Hah. And so, that's the kind of thing. *And I said, "Kevin, quit trying to control me.* Just, if you want to talk to me, come and talk to me when I'm sitting in the car and starting the car." So that's sort of an example of what I call control. [Are there any particular situations in which the control would lead to the violence?] Yeah. *Those are examples of what the control issue starts.* I mean, that's how it starts. And then, if it were to lead to violence, that same potential situation would continue to escalate. And so, that was what was sporadic about it is I couldn't ever tell which time. I mean, if he were in a different frame of mind, now, even that, he would have run down the alley, grabbed me by the arm and said, "I told you to come back." But he hasn't done that. He got really upset with me the other night. Another situation of, "Come here and talk to me." I said, "Kevin, I'm doing something else." "Don't leave the room." "Kevin, I am sorry but," I don't know what I was doing. I think it was the dirty clothes or something. I was going about my business. That really bothers him to talk to me and not have me setting down and talking straight to him. And that really bothers him for some reason, me mobile. *And I feel like it's threatening or challenging to him. Maybe it's not.* [Why would it be threatening or challenging to him?] I'm not sure, but that's the impression that I get. *Of, "I told you to do something and you're supposed to do it." And I say, "Hey, I'm your equal and I don't have to do it."* So that's the kind of scenario that's set up. [Emphasis added.]

Kevin had discussed the theme of "giving in" in prior interviews. He addresses the notion of "not giving ground" in detail, suggesting that letting Lisa have her way would mean losing power and submitting to her control. But Lisa would challenge his decision of how to handle an argument. In the past, she would abide by his decision (for example, to settle the argument later) or violence would result. Kevin notes that he had to deal with Lisa's challenge in another way, that is, walk away (apparently giving up control) as opposed to using violence.

Lisa provides two instances in which Kevin demanded that she behave in a particular way, specifically to stop whatever she was doing and give him her full attention. She does admit that she was challenging him and that, before, that challenge would have escalated into violence. However, she believes that because she is Kevin's equal, he does not have the right to tell her what to do.

The events leading up to a possible incident involve the woman's challenge to the man's right to control the situation. As mentioned in previous chapters, issues of control often precipitated a violent incident. Here, in the case of Lisa and Kevin, Lisa was challenging Kevin's right to tell her what to do.

It is important to point out that in this first stage, although a woman may not overtly challenge her partner's control, he may *interpret* her behavior as a challenge. In this sense, the man feels that his power is threatened even though there may be no basis for it. Therefore, sometimes violence may erupt, not because of anything that the woman does, but because of what the man perceives the woman to be doing.

STAGE TWO: LOSING CONTROL AND USING VIOLENCE TO REGAIN CONTROL

A batterer may feel out of control when a situation is not going the way he wants it to go. A way to get back into control is to use violence. For example, Ronald said in our third interview:

So I've got, supposedly in control of the situation and I haven't been yet, so dammit, I'll take control. "Boom." Yeah.

Part of this out of control feeling is related to the fact that the man wants his partner to behave in a specific way, and when that is challenged, he feels threatened and fears that he no longer is in control of the situation. He responds violently, as response to his perception, feeling, and fear, because he has learned that violence helps him regain control over his mate. The mechanisms that are at work are best described by Kevin in our third interview:

Well, let me give you the boiling teapot thing. Ha. It's like, all these things are the fire under the teapot. And if you leave the fire there long enough, it's going to boil. And when it's boiling it's unstable. Anything can happen. *So the only way you can make it quit boiling is to get things into control. That means either leave the situation or force the situation to stop.* Now, when this one happened, I left the situation. I went away from where the fire was. Okay? And I just walked off and gave myself time to relax and calm down and then I came back. *And the other alternative is that you try to use physical force to make those people submit to you.* And you say, "Okay. Leave me alone." And you actually drive them away. [Emphasis added.]

Kevin is saying that issues come up that individuals often do not agree on. If an agreement is not reached, it can lead to a dangerous situation where violence can happen. It is a dangerous situation because the batterer realizes that he is not able to get the other to act as he would want her to act. She is challenging his decision of how she is to act. To resolve the problem, the batterer can leave the situation in which the disagreement resides and settle the issue later, when they are both calmer, or he can force the other to submit to his original decision through physical means. In either case, he is attempting to regain control of a situation that appeared to be out of control.

In my second interview with Mike, he said something that I think highlights the dynamics of instrumental control:

But I think a lot of the violence that men have is because they cannot physically control something. I mean, without abuse. Like I can control a situation, I can control, how do I put it, I can control how I'm going to say something to you. But I can't control what you say back. So I guess the only way I can control that is by stopping you from doing it all together.

Mike explains that while he had control over how he acted, he did not have control over how Kay reacted. He used physical abuse as a mechanism for controlling her reaction.

STAGE THREE: REGAINING CONTROL THROUGH THE OTHER'S SUBMISSION

Interviews with the respondents suggest that one of the reasons batterers choose a violent as opposed to nonviolent form of conflict resolution is because the negative consequences they experience for behaving violently are minimized. Although the batterers may feel guilty for behaving violently towards their partners, they are quickly relieved of this guilt when the women forgive them or take the blame for the violence. Additionally, the batterers know that they will not be severely punished for their violence because if the women hit back, they generally will not hurt the batterers to the degree that the men have hurt them. The women are often physically weaker. Furthermore, the men's violence often results in successfully forcing their partners to submit to their control. The women typically react by giving into what the batterers want. Two couples, Mike and Kay, and Doug and Wendy, help illustrate the dynamics that are involved. In our last interview, Mike remarked:

I feel like the violence in the past has been because of my insecurity. *I couldn't beat anyone else up, so then when I got angry, I had to take it out on my family.* . . . I honestly don't know. Like I said earlier, I think a lot of that was the insecurity knowing that *she was the only type of person that I could beat up.* [Emphasis added.]

And Kay said in our first interview:

[How did you respond to him when he had done that?] Well I couldn't believe it. *After he had slapped me and everything, he said, "We're getting a divorce."* And he ran out the door. Slammed the door. And I sat there, and I cried. I couldn't believe it. See, I had been married so many times before, and I felt like I had to make this marriage work. Three-time loser, failure. I thought, "Gosh. I can't let this happen again." *So when he came back I begged, pleaded with him, "Don't, please don't leave. Please. I'm sorry. I didn't mean to. I didn't mean to make you mad."* And everything because I was just, "Oh, please. I don't want this to happen to me again." And he just went off, and then he came back. "Well, I guess we'll work at things." *And it seemed like one thing after another after that.* [Emphasis added.]

Mike admits that he could not beat up anyone else. Kay did not want to fail in another marriage. Moreover, she wanted to have more children, and Mike seemed to want that too. When he was violent several months after they were married and threatened divorce, she felt that her hope for finally succeeding at marriage had ended. Out of desperation, she frantically apologized for what she had done and pleaded with him not to leave. The fact that "one thing happened after another after that" suggests that Mike continued to be violent because the negative consequences for behaving violently were minimized. It was not until she left him in March 1985 that he stopped being violent. It is unclear whether Mike stopped being violent because Kay was no longer living with him and therefore he did not have anyone to hit or because Kay's leaving made Mike want to stop being violent.

In my first interview with Doug, he said this:

I never thought of myself as just looking for a fight. But in relationships with women, I found myself looking for, *if she says something, or after it gets this bad then I'm going to cream her, and I would.* [Emphasis added.]

In my first interview with Wendy, she said:

[How would you typically respond when that would happen? How would you react?] To the violence? [Mm. Hmm.] The initial, of course, was to cry, or whatever. And then I would just kind of draw into myself. *I guess I became submissive. I was real careful not to do anything or not say anything that I thought was going to upset him and to do as much as I could that I thought he'd like or appreciate or whatever.* [Afterwards, in the following days, or just immediately?] I guess pretty much immediately cause if we'd been bickering, I would shut up. I wouldn't say anything. It was just kind of like, I would breathe, I didn't know what to do. I'd just kind of retreat into myself and *not do anything that I thought was going to upset him.* [Emphasis added.]

Doug indicates that he typically found himself looking for a fight with women. From Wendy's account, Doug's violence was successful in getting Wendy to submit to him. She was careful not to do anything that she felt might upset him, and she did as much as she could to please him. In my last interview with Wendy, she said this:

[Why do you think men do that, Wendy?] I think, it's something that they need to do to prove that they're a man and that they're strong by beating up on somebody that's weaker than them. Doug has never hit a man. *And I think that he's afraid to have a fight with a man for fear that he'll get beat up, but he knows he can beat up women and he's not going to get hurt.* [Emphasis added.]

Wendy notes that Doug was successful in controlling her because he knew that she could not hurt him. She was an easy target. This is not to suggest that the fault for Doug's violence lies with Wendy.

INSTRUMENTAL VIOLENCE: A WAY OF DOING POWER

The men want to direct and determine how their partner behaves, and the way that they do this is through violence. If the women do not behave in the expected fashion, conflict arises, and violence is used to "get control." The data support the fact that the men use violence to dominate, control, and force the women to conform to what they want. This is exemplified in Mike's and Kay's descriptions. For example, Mike said in our second interview:

[But why would you hit her if she was going to be all the emotional support that you would have?] *Simply because she wasn't seeing things the way that I would.* I wanted her to fall into a role model, but if she got out of that role model, that's not what I wanted. I had broke the security. *I guess the only way that I could get her back in line was to hit her.* . . . [Why do you think the physical abuse came up then, later?] Well, like I said before, *it was just a way to get her to conform to what I wanted.* [Emphasis added.]

Kay said in our initial interview:

I had no control over things. He wanted to control everything. He didn't want me to control anything. He wouldn't allow me to control anything. [Emphasis added.]

Then, in our second interview she said:

He's the type of person that I could not make a decision for myself. *If I decided to cut my hair and went ahead and did it, I would get into a lot of trouble.* He would really get angry. If I decided that it was okay for the child to spend the night with a friend, he didn't like it. I didn't ask him first. If I go to the grocery store and I take a little bit longer than what I should have, he didn't like it because I was supposed to be where he wanted me to be at the exact time. *I wasn't supposed to do anything that I wasn't told to do.* [Emphasis added.]

Mike indicates that when Kay did not conform to his expectations, he would use violence. Kay says that she had absolutely no control over her life, that Mike held that control. In her second excerpt, she shows how Mike controlled her in the areas of physical appearance, management of the children, or household duties. In each case, she could not act independently of Mike. Therefore, it appears that Mike had a great deal of power over Kay.

Violence is a way of "doing power" in a relationship. Henry and Jackie support this notion. Henry said:

At this point, she had decided that our relationship, I wanted power, and it was a power struggle, and I wanted to be in control and everything. I wanted to be in control, and she wouldn't submit to that, and so she thought everything was a result of control and me trying to have it. Like, when I decided I wanted to talk to her, and then I didn't. And she didn't. She decided she was going to make her last stand at my house to prove that she didn't have to submit to my control. In other words, I told her to get out, and she was not going to leave my house. [What do you think of that interpretation?] *I think that there were many times in the last few months of our relationship where I wanted to control things.* But I think she decided that the interpretation stretched back to many months. Not just in the months when we had violence or when things were getting bad. *I think she decided that I had controlled my younger brother. I just wanted to be in control, that I wanted to kind of be chauvinistic, old-fashioned and sexist and I just wanted to control the relationship and I didn't like her. We weren't getting along because she stood up to me and wanted to share equally in power. But, I think that there was some truth to the power problem. I used to tell her, "If you can't call, I've got it." I used to draw lines, and I expected her to give me some sort of respect because maybe I was the man but maybe because I was a partner, and I just didn't think I was getting any respect.* [Emphasis added.]

Jackie said this:

He became this fictitious male and thought that he should have control and was dominant and I should do what he told me to do and what he said. And I'm a real fighter. [Emphasis added.]

Henry indicates that Jackie felt that he wanted power and the right to control things. He believes that she may have had a point. Jackie mentions that Henry thought he should have control and dominance. However, the fact that she indicates that she was a "fighter" implies that she was not going to put up with that. Henry even mentions how she challenged his control.

It is important to reiterate that the use of violence to control may arise and continue, in part, because the batterer learns that violence can be used successfully as a means to maintain control over his partner, because he does not incur negative repercussions for using it. Early in a relationship, control may be an unintended consequence of behaving violently. Through learning, however, it may eventually become an intended consequence.

Let me now turn to the second phase that characterizes the violence over time, that is, the movement from instrumental violent behavior to nonviolent behavior. Then, I will discuss the two phases in terms of the symbolic interaction model that was presented in Chapter 5.

Phase Two: Instrumental Violence to Nonviolence Through Control

Over time, when respondents reflected on whether or not violence still existed in their relationships, they typically discussed it in terms of whether the batterer had changed. If they recognized a change in the batterer, then they believed that this change brought about nonviolence in their relationships. If they saw no change, then it was highly likely that they indicated that their relationships were still violent. Almost half of the respondents described the nature of this change in terms of whether the men could (*a*) control their anger, (*b*) control their violent behavior, and (*c*) avoid controlling their partner. As will be shown in the findings, this change is a function of a changing self. Specifically, the expectations of the self change with respect to one's emotions, behavior, and attitude towards the other.

Before addressing these findings, let me first discuss the subsample of respondents used in this analysis. Because longitudinal data was not obtained from all the respondents, information regarding change was limited to a select group of respondents. As Henry and Jackie agreed to only one interview, I was not able to obtain data on the aspect of change. Fred is also omitted from analysis because he decided to leave the research study after our second interview; due to such limited information from him, the element of change could not be captured.

Those individuals who did not talk about the men's change in self in terms of control, and thus, did not move to nonviolence, included Ann, Ronald and Kathy, Doug and Wendy, and Bill. What these individuals have in common is that their relationships ended at some point during the time I was conducting the interviews. This suggests that there may be some link between the men's change in self in terms of control, the probability of violence continuing, and a relationship remaining intact.

Those respondents who invoked the notion of control to explain how the men had changed, and thus moved toward nonviolence, included Mike and Kay, Larry and Terri, Kevin and Lisa, and Frank. In all of these relationships, though the couple separated for a period of time, they eventually reunited. Nancy mentioned Frank changing only in our third interview, but she did not discuss it in terms of control. Later, I will explain why this occurred.

CONTROLLING EMOTIONS

In Chapter 4, I indicated that the men felt that their emotions were out of control. As the women did not make reference to the men's emotions in terms of control, it was not possible to compare the partners' perspectives regarding the relationship between control and emotions. Rather, the men's perspectives were the focus, highlighting how the notion of control was invoked.

As the women did not discuss their partners' emotions in terms of control, one would expect that they would also not discuss a change in their partner in terms of controlling their emotions. This is what was found. When the women referred to a change in their partner, it was not in the realm of emotions. They did discuss a change in the other in terms of their behavior. This will be discussed in the next section.

Mike, Larry, Kevin, and Frank perceived a change in themselves by way of attempting to control their emotions. Therefore, there was a change in how they viewed the emotional aspect of themselves. This, in turn, contributed to a movement toward nonviolence. For example, in our second interview, Larry said this about his emotions:

I think a lot of my rage has been powerlessness over situations and an ability to accept the situations or that powerlessness. Feeling trapped. But just nonacceptance. Real intense, absolute nonacceptance of things that are going to be that way. No matter what. And just can't accept that they're going to be that way. But I don't know. I had it forever. And certainly growing up with an asshole for a father, that's a pretty powerless situation. And it's pretty fucking hard to accept. . . . I think I've hit some milestones. Some conscious realizations in the last couple of months. I don't think I was doing any less change before. [Milestones? Like what?] *Well, like realizing that I do an awful lot of mental fighting and that it's just really nonacceptance in that I don't want to do it any more. That's a milestone, but it didn't just occur in the last couple of months. That realization occurred in the last couple of months but the process leading up to that realization has been going on, in a pure sense, my entire life. I mean, ever since I started pushing, mentally fighting people that began the path of getting to the place where I got tired of mentally fighting Terri.* [Emphasis added.]

Then, in our third interview, Larry said:

I think I'm getting better for the first time. [In what way?] In that there are a lot of things, maybe I just stuffed it, and it's coming out (ha) now. He-he. And you can say, "Here." *Six months ago or two years ago, if I would have been in the same situation on Thursday or on Friday with Terri, almost every time she was being unreasonable, I would have gotten angry.* I mean, verbally raised my voice and had gotten physically bigger if I could. I don't know how I do that, but my sponsor tells me I do that. He said when I get scared, I get bigger. Louder. And I didn't do that in a very large proportion of the time at all until eventually I started. But even in the four hours of argument, there was a lot of frustration that I felt that wasn't going to do it her. Just yelling at her. *And so we managed just to talk.* [Emphasis added.]

In our second interview, Larry claims that his rage was a result of feeling powerless over situations. Feeling trapped and unable to accept a situation as it was, he would get angry. Towards the end of this interview, he indicates that his nonacceptance of situations has resulted in mental fighting with others, including Terri, his partner, and that he does not want it any more. Moreover, he indicates that while this change in himself occurred only recently, the process leading up to this change has been occurring all his life.

It appears that Larry's method of dealing with his anger changes along with his changing self. Before, every time he thought Terri was being unreasonable, he would get angry and yell. Now, they talk things out. He implies that he is now controlling his anger.

Therefore, some batterers are beginning to learn how to manage their emotions (Hochschild, 1983). Moreover, the fact that they believe, over time, that they have to control their emotions supports the fact that they view their emotions as out of control when they are violent, as discussed in Chapter 4. Specifically, there would be no cause for them to say that they need to control their emotions had they not believed that their emotions were out of control to begin with.

CONTROLLING VIOLENT BEHAVIOR

Another area where control was linked to a change in the men, and thus a movement toward nonviolence, was when both the men *and* women discussed how the man's behavior, over time, became nonviolent in nature. Kevin and Lisa provide an example of this. Kevin said in our third interview:

I remember telling her, I said, "*I feel like I'm losing control.*" I said, "Right at that point." And she said, "Well, go outside and go for a walk. Just get out of the house." *So I just went outside and I walked about six blocks, and I came back in and I was fine.* [Emphasis added.]

Lisa said in our third interview:

But it's getting even better. I do not feel he has the need. Even when things are out of control in his own life, I don't sense him feeling he needs to control the home as much as he used to. So, I don't know if it's circumstances are getting better or his way of dealing with it is getting better. What makes me say this, recently we had an incident. This was this weekend. Everybody was tired. The kids are this. The phone went dead. And we couldn't find the phone bill and I couldn't remember what day. I thought, my gosh, they've cut the phone off. And I couldn't find the phone bill. And so everybody was getting upset. The kids hadn't eaten yet. There was this, "Nanannana." And, "The phone's dead? Did you pay the phone bill?" "No. Did you pay the phone bill?" "No. No. No. No." And so, he was getting really upset, and he was sure the phone was dead because I didn't pay the phone bill. They cut the phone off. Which was not the case. But we couldn't find the phone. And, in effect, the phone was dead for three days. We just fixed it today. *But, he said, "Lisa, I'm losing control."* He said, "Why can't you just reach out to me and help me get control of the situation." I said, "Kevin, I've got my own problems right now." I was trying to deal with this little crisis. *And, he said, "But I really feel like I'm getting violent." I said, "Then leave. Just leave."* And then he made some sort of smart remark or something. *And he did. Which surprised me. He did, and he went and walked around the block.* He went to a phone booth to call our phone to see what they were going say. "This phone has been temporarily disconnected." Hah. Or, "This phone is under repair." And he found out it was being repaired. And so, then he came back, and the pizza had arrived. The kids were happy. And I said, "Are you feeling better now?" And he said, "Yeah. Much." He said, "That really helped me to get away." [Emphasis added.]

In Kevin's excerpt, he mentions that when he felt that he was losing control, he left the situation. Kevin had a long history of being violent to Lisa, but instead of using physical violence as a response to how he was feeling in the situation, he walked away, thus controlling his impulse to strike out.

Lisa provides a more detailed description of what happened. What is noteworthy is that she also mentions this event and makes the same point, that is, that Kevin controlled his violent response by walking away. This surprised Lisa, probably because she did not think he would take her advice and leave, but that he instead would respond violently. She does note early on that she thinks Kevin may be getting better in terms of dealing with his violence. Therefore, both Kevin and Lisa highlight the fact that Kevin controlled his behavior when the alternative (using violence) may have been more likely to occur given Kevin's history of being violent.

It is important to point out that a change in the self regarding how violence should be perceived, that is, viewing violence as inappropriate, is directly related to the men controlling their behavior. Kevin and Lisa exemplify this change in Kevin in the following excerpts. Kevin said in our third interview:

[What do you think makes men come to the point of stopping their violence?] Well, I think you've got to want to. And I mean really, consciously and morally want to. And there's a lot more in that statement than just the words because it's like an alcoholic or a drug addict or any other person that has that kind of a disease. The alcoholic can wake up every morning with a hangover and say, "I don't want to drink any more." And he probably really doesn't want to, but what he's really saying is, "I don't want to feel the way I feel." It's not that he's really internally sorry for the fact that he was intoxicated again or that the drug addict had pumped heroin again or something. He's upset because of what he's going through as a result of his actions. And it was the same thing with me. Until this last time. I was sorry. It was like a kid being sorry he got caught. Well, he got caught. If he'd never got caught, he might go on stealing or whatever he was doing the rest of his life. Well, step two [inaudible], he was sorry he got caught. He wasn't sorry for what he had done and really wanted to change. He was sorry he got caught. [What do you mean by sorry he got caught?] Well, in the past when I was sorry about, and I'm using the word sorry as a remorseful type word. Okay? When I was sorry about the fact that I had gotten in a fight with Lisa, I wasn't really sorry that I had hurt her or that I had caused fear and pain and had suppressed her. That really wasn't why I was sorry. What I was sorry was that I had again hit her and then I had to live with that guilt inside me as a result of my actions. I had no regard at all for what I had really done to her. I was just remorseful that I had done it and it was causing pain on me. Now this last time, I really came to the point, after I read this book, I really came to the point, "Hey, you've got to be sorry for what you've done to her." My remorse will go away if I don't hurt her. But, yet I've got to be sorry for her, not for me. And I've got to want to quit because of her or what I'm doing to her and quit thinking about me. Instead of turning everything inward, I had to look at what I was doing on the outside. That's why I say, the first thing is, the man's got to be truly sorry for what he's doing. And he's got to truly want to change. Not because of what it inflicts on himself, but for what he's doing to the people around him. And that was my first step to recovery. Once I did that, then I was able to go to Lisa and I was able to sit there and say, "For years, I've been wrong." "Not you. I have." . . . They have to come to the point that they sit down and they say, "Hey, I am a wife abuser and what I'm doing is wrong. Now why am I doing this?" And then go to that person and sit there and let them unload.

Lisa said in our third interview:

One of the changes for us was Kevin really finally admitting, yes, this is a problem for him. Because of his mind, good Christian men don't do things like this. So, I just can't admit that there would be a real problem with it. It was liking drinking. [Inaudible.] So I think admitting to himself that yes this is a situation. See, when we were in the Navy, he couldn't admit it or his career would be down the drain. He just could not admit a lot of things about himself. Because of what they have to maintain. You just don't do certain things, and it was a problem for him, and he couldn't admit it to anybody. He couldn't turn to anyone for it. Or he felt like he couldn't. There's a possibility he could have reached out for some help and probably gotten it. But, in his mind, he couldn't. He wouldn't allow himself to do that.

Both Kevin and Lisa indicate how Kevin's view of violence changed. Kevin claims that any sorrow he experienced before for his violent behavior was not because he had hurt Lisa, but rather because he had hit her again and had to live with the guilt. He now realizes that he has to stop thinking about himself and think about what he is doing to Lisa. Only then can he change. Lisa notes that one of the changes in their relationship was Kevin admitting that he had a problem with violence. Previously, he could not admit that or seek help. Therefore, I would argue that the reason Kevin was behaving nonviolently was directly related to a change in himself regarding the appropriateness of violence.

Avoiding Controlling the Woman

A third way in which the men change and move toward nonviolence is by making an effort not to control their partner. This is best illustrated in the excerpts below from Mike and Kay. Mike said in our second interview:

I expected her to play the mother that I never had. Someone that stayed home and took care of the kids. Had dinner ready and kept the house clean. But in expecting that, I realize now that I, what I had done is I took her personality away from her. *I wouldn't let her see friends. I wouldn't let her go do things that she needed to be doing. I didn't let her take time for herself. And I'm doing that exactly right now.* [Emphasis added.]

In our last interview, Mike remarked:

I've come down to the theory, I've got control over myself. She's got control over herself. Together we've got to control the family. And that's not the way it used to be. *She can't be happy if I'm controlling her.* And I couldn't be happy for her to control me. [Do you think that she controlled you in the past?] Nope. She's never given me the chance to cause *I've controlled her. And I don't want any more of that.* [Emphasis added.]

Kay said in our second interview:

Well, he's excited. *He's letting me do things that I didn't used to be able to do.* He always complained that I wasn't a woman. But yet at the same time, he didn't want me to do any of the things that women do. Like, [inaudible] buying me some cosmetics or getting my hair done or doing any of this stuff, and now he takes me to the city, to the French Connection for my birthday, and lets me buy some cologne, custom just made for me. And he gets a thrill out of seeing me happy now. He draws happiness from seeing me happy. So I think it's going to work, and I think he's going to be fine. [Emphasis added.]

Mike implies in his first excerpt that he controlled Kay by not permitting her to do things for herself. He said that he was letting her do those things now. In the second excerpt, he claims that he controlled Kay and that he doesn't want to do that any more. This suggests that Mike's self was changing with respect to controlling Kay. Kay's excerpt verifies the fact that Mike was letting her do things she was not permitted to do before. Therefore, Mike was avoiding controlling Kay.

Control, Violence, and Change Over Time

There are at least three stages that characterize instrumental violence over time. Control is implicated in this three-stage process. A woman challenges the man's right to control her (or the man perceives her behavior as challenging his control), the man feels a temporary loss of control and uses violence to regain control, and the man successfully regains control when the woman inevitably submits to him. The stages are embedded in the stages of the act discussed in Chapter 4.

First, the woman's challenge or threat to the man's right to control initiates the impulse stage of the violent act. The immediate reaction (from the "I") is to behave aggressively. The man feels under attack and out of control. The form of violence that has been planned (in the perception stage) is then executed (by the "I") signalling the manipulation stage of the act. The motive behind this violence is to regain control. After the violence has consummated, the woman typically responds by submitting to the man, thereby reinforcing the violence. The man sees that the violence has successfully enabled him to regain control. He maintains that control until the woman challenges him again, thereby repeating the cycle of violence.

The movement from violence to nonviolence reveals itself in three ways. Physical violence seems to disappear in the relationship for those men who are able to (*a*) control their anger in the sense that they identify and attempt to keep in check those things that are likely to get them angry, (*b*) control their violence, for example, walk away when a conflict situation arises, and (*c*) avoid controlling their partner. Moreover, changes in the expectations of the self accompany changes emotionally, behaviorally, and with regard to the other.

It is important to note that when we interpret a relationship as changing from violence to nonviolence as a function of the man changing, this interpretation must come from examining all the information available on the thoughts, feelings, and events that occur in the relationship from both the man and woman's perspective. For example, in the case of Frank and Nancy, I found that while the relationship appeared to be moving toward nonviolence, appearances were deceiving. Only after I examined all the data available from both perspectives was I able to see why. It is useful to discuss this relationship at some length in order to show that one must be cautious in making interpretations about nonviolence in a relationship.

In my third and fourth interviews with Frank, he discussed how he was controlling his behavior and avoiding any control over Nancy. As he said in our third interview:

And I said, "I'm not going to play any games." And I pointed out to her, I said, "I've been playing games with you, and I realize that, and I'm not going to do it any more. *I cannot control you.* I'm not going to make your decisions for you. You're going to have to make your own. And these are the things that I'm going to do, and that's it. Whether you're here or not. I've got to do them. I've got a problem with violence and I want to do something about it. And nobody, not even you, are going to intervene to make me change my mind, or I feel that you're going to provoke me to change my mind, cause I know it's all me and no one else. *And I make that decision when I become violent. I'm doing things and learning things to deter those things.* And, when I feel that you come in between that or you become, something that triggers those things, I'll totally ignore. *I'm going to go through whatever sources I have learned to deter those things.*" [Emphasis added.]

Then, in our fourth interview, Frank said:

[One of things that you said is that you understand why you are violent?] Mm. Hmm. [Now why is that?] Because I choose to be. I'm frustrated and the only thing

I want to do is [inaudible]. That was one alternative. Now I'm finding out that I don't need to strike out. Just not accept the responsibility, basically. Accept what I do and be truthful with myself and *accept the fact that I'm not going to change Nancy.* I'm not going to change anybody else for that matter. *Either walk away or talk to someone or just consider the issue as not important.* And before, I've always kept those things in. I felt that it was my responsibility. I took responsibility. And as an end result, totally confusion. It made me more aggressive to want to fight. Or strike to change. And now I feel that it wasn't and it's not necessary to do those things. Just to withdraw myself from the situation first of all. [Emphasis added.]

In Frank's first excerpt, he indicates he cannot control Nancy. He admits that he is responsible for being violent and that he is learning to control his behavior, for example, ignoring whatever triggers him to be violent. In the second excerpt, he again mentions that he cannot control Nancy by saying that he cannot change her. Further, he again says that he is learning to control his behavior by walking away, talking to someone, or considering the issue that causes the conflict as not important.

However, there is more to this relationship than what the previous excerpts suggest. In our third interview, Frank also said this:

And the conversation came up, and I said, "Leslie is causing us a problem." I said, "To be quite honest with you, if you don't really ask Leslie to just step away, I'm not asking you to cut your friendship off with it, I'm just asking you to just have her not come around as often. To keep her distance away from us until we get our lives together, and then you can go back to her." Well, she feels that's a threat. She feels she doesn't want to do that, *that I'm going to want to control her.* And that's why I said, "Okay, well, I'm sorry. You understand what I'm asking for?" [Emphasis added.]

On the surface, this may appear to be a reasonable request that Frank made, that is, that Nancy not see her friend, Leslie. However, it must be understood that Frank and Nancy constantly argued over whether Nancy could have friends. Frank always seemed to find a justification for Nancy not to have them. Early on, he indicated that she shouldn't be out with her friends because she needed to be home with her children. Here, he notes that it is because they needed some time together. In my conversations with Nancy, she indicated that Frank was jealous of her close friendships. He went so far as to not take her places where he thought her friends would be. Though Nancy had a need for female friendships, she indicated that, because of Frank's insistence that she not see her friends, she ended up losing all but one, that being Leslie. Now Frank was telling her not to see Leslie.

Despite Nancy's disagreement over not seeing Leslie, she went along with Frank's request. She wanted their relationship to work and felt that if that was what it took, she would agree to what Frank wanted. As she said in our third interview:

But, see, Leslie, every time she calls or comes over, Frank has a fit. Until finally I had to tell her that her and I couldn't be friends until Frank and I got our lives together.

So I did tell her that last week. Because he was throwing a fit over her every time she came over. . . . [How do you feel about not going out with Leslie and not having friends?] I don't like the idea, but I want to give this relationship my best shot. My all. Everything I can do. And, like I told him, if my all isn't good enough, then what else have I got [inaudible]. Then I don't have anything back from it. If he really feels like, and maybe it will, okay? Maybe Leslie does have a little bit of an influence on our relationship. So, if I can get rid of all the outside interference and just deal on our relationship all together, maybe we can get it together. [Emphasis added.]

Frank appeared to still be controlling Nancy. If Frank was controlling his own behavior, one would expect that he would remain nonviolent. However, in my last interview with Nancy, she told me of a severe violent incident that had occurred a few days prior. Moreover, Frank's control over her reappeared. Frank would not even let her leave the house. As she said:

It's like I've been getting really depressed. And then I start getting physical things wrong with me. I know that it's only from stress, and I know when I get sick, it's like I get real pale and stuff. And I know I'm not sick. *It's just sitting in the house everyday. I just hate it.* [Emphasis added.]

What a batterer says about control cannot necessarily be taken at face value. All the evidence must be accumulated, including the woman's accounts. Frank's discrepancy in what he says as opposed to what he does may be due to the fact that behavioral change may be lagging behind attitudinal change. In time, it is possible that Frank could behave nonviolently and not want to control his partner.

Though I argued that, over time, violence becomes instrumental, it is not purely instrumental. This is suggested by the fact that a movement toward nonviolence is accompanied by a batterer managing his emotional and behavioral responses to the degree that violence is inhibited. However, it still has an impulsive element to it. Additionally, recall that the violent act begins with an impulse to aggress. It is likely that the batterers not only learn that violence can be used as a means to control the other, but also that they can expect themselves to respond impulsively when they feel threatened or under attack. Therefore, on one level, while instrumentality characterizes the violence over time, on another level, the impulsive nature of the violence still exists.

As mentioned in the beginning of this chapter, control assumed two different meanings as object. While control was understood with reference to the other, and thus had to do with an external process in that it dealt with how the woman (and not the batterer) should or should not behave, control was also described in terms of the batterer's ability to manage his emotions and behavior, thus referring to control as an internal process. This is directly related to the instrumental and impulsive natures of violence, respectively. Control as an external process related to the violence as instrumental, while control as an internal process related to violence as impulsive.

It is important to realize that when there was a movement toward non-violence, the instrumental (control as an external process) and impulsive (control as an internal process) aspects of violence were addressed. As the batterers were learning how to control their emotions and behavior, they were thereby attending to their impulsive responses. Additionally, through learning that one person should not control another, especially when that control takes the form of violence, the batterers were addressing the instrumental nature of their violence.

Summary

A symbolic interactionist model of domestic violence was presented in Chapter 5 in order to make sense of respondents' perceptions that the batterers' emotions are out of control and that their behavior is both in and out of control when they are violent. The underlying process of violence was explained in terms of control, the stages of the violent act, and the relevance of the "I" and "Me" of the self. Chapter 6 presented detail evidence from the data on how the model operates. The expectations of the "Me" to be violent or nonviolent largely influences whether one will carry out the impulse to aggress, carry out the impulse but do so with some control, or inhibit the impulse to aggress.

This chapter examines violence over time and thus completes the picture of how the model operates. Apparently, over time, violence tends to stop when the batterers consciously control their emotions and violent behavior and stop controlling their partners. In this way, the batterers address both the impulsive and instrumental aspects of their violence. However, a change in the batterers is intimately connected to a change in themselves. When the expectations of the "Me" (more specifically, the expectations of the self) change, so too does behavior. Therefore, an inner movement towards nonviolence is met with an outer behavioral change. The reason for the change in self-expectations is unclear. It is likely that the reasons may be several—for example, participation in therapy, time, or one's own motivation. What is most important is that the impact of the expectations of the "Me," over time, continue to have an influence.

It was also found that the violent act is carried out over time, not only to satiate the impulse to aggress but also to maintain control over the woman. Instrumental violence appears and reappears primarily through the mechanism of learning. The expectations of the "Me" are to be violent and will remain so until they undergo a change. Until this change occurs, it is assumed that violence will continue.

8
Conclusions

Domestic violence continues to be a serious social problem in our society. Though there is evidence that within the past ten years there has been a decrease in husband-to-wife violence, the decrease is small, with approximately 1.6 million wives still experiencing abuse (Straus & Gelles, 1986). Early in this book, I indicated that we need to understand the nature (dynamics) of violence in relationships and that in order to do this, we should analyze violence as part of an ongoing interaction. By conducting longitudinal, in-depth interviews, with men *and* women involved in violent relationships, this research has attempted to identify the processual nature of violence over time. Having found the notion of control as a central and reoccurring theme in descriptions of violent behavior, I have explained how control relates to violence by generating a symbolic interaction model of domestic violence.

Before discussing the general implications of this research, and future concerns for symbolic interactionists, let me briefly review the findings from this study. In addition, I will discuss, in detail, how the men's and women's perspectives are to be understood, given that both viewpoints were examined in this research. Future research needs to incorporate both perspectives in order to fully understand the dynamics of battering.

Summary of Research Findings

This study revealed that the object respondents focused on, rendering it meaningful, was the notion of control. It was invoked in order to understand the existence and continuation of violence. When violence no longer became a consistent feature of a relationship, the notion of control was again invoked to explain why a man stopped being violent.

In Chapter 4, I showed that respondents viewed the batterers' emotions as out of control and their behavior as both in *and* out of their control when violence occurred. Using the symbolic interactionist perspective in Chapter 5, I explained the process of violence and its relationship to emotional and behavioral control in terms of the four stages of the violent act and the relevance of the "I" and and "Me."

In the first stage of the violent act, a contextual cue, specifically conflict over control, serves to initiate a spontaneous impulse to aggress. The "I," the subjective and nonreflective aspect of the self, responds. In the perception stage, the woman stands out as a distant object. The batterer focuses attention on her and decides upon a line of action with reference to her. The "Me" is called forth in the planning and construction of the action, and thereby gives direction to the "I." I noted that the perception stage may be a critical point in the violent act because the content of the "Me," that is, whether the batterer thinks that others expect him to respond violently, will influence his behavior.

After a line of action is chosen, manipulation takes place. The specific form of violence that was planned in the perception stage is now administered by the "I," under the guidance of the "Me." The data revealed that one might carry out the impulse to aggress, carry out the impulse but with some control, or inhibit the impulse to aggress. I argued that a batterer may carry out the impulse to aggress but do so with some control, because the "Me" may interrupt the actions of the "I" in the manipulation stage, making batterers consciously aware of their violence. Therefore, the impulse to aggress is monitored and perhaps moderated. Finally, consummation occurs when the violence has ended and the impulse to aggress has been acted upon. The "Me" reappears to interpret the situation and evaluates whether the act has been completed.

Descriptions of the violence as out of control in terms of emotions, and in or out of control in terms of behavior, can exist simultaneously. While the violent act may be set in motion with the impulse to aggress (through the "I"), it also may be carried out and completed with some degree of control (through the "Me"). In this case, emotions would be viewed as out of control and behavior would be viewed as in control. If the impulse to aggress is carried out without interruption from the "Me" in the manipulation stage, then the view that emotions and behavior are out of control would appear. Therefore, the violent act, upon reflection, has both uncontrollable (impulsive) and controllable (instrumental) elements.

The basis of the symbolic interactionist model of violence was illustrated in Chapter 6. Evidence from the data on the interactionist perspective came largely from detailed descriptions of violent incidents provided by the men. It was shown how the different expectations of the "Me" in the perception stage related to the various responses a batterer might make in the manipulation stage.

Finally, the longitudinal nature of the violence was examined in Chapter 7. I found that two general phases characterize the violence over time. In the first phase, violence emerges in a relationship and eventually takes on an instrumental flavor. In the second phase, there is a movement to nonviolence when the men place the violence under their control. In the first phase, when a man is first violent, his violence is carried out primarily to satiate the impulse to aggress. Hence, early battering is indicative of wanting to strike back at another. Over time and through learning, however, the violence becomes instrumental: that is, carried out in order to control the woman. To understand the nature of instrumental violence, I identified and discussed three stages that helped describe the dynamics that are involved. These included (a) challenging the right to control the other, (b) losing control and using violence to regain control, and (c) regaining control through the other's submission.

The three stages of instrumental violence can be understood in terms of the stages of the act. The woman's *challenge* to the man's *right to control* (or, the man *interpreting* the woman's behavior as threatening his power) signals the impulse stage of the violent act. The man feels under attack and out of control. In the perception stage, he decides upon the specific form of violence he will use on the woman. Execution of the violence signals the manipulation stage. The motive behind the violence is to regain control. After the violence has been consummated, the woman typically responds by submitting to the man, thereby reinforcing the violence. The man sees that the violence has successfully enabled him to regain control. He maintains that control until the woman challenges him again, and the cycle of violence is repeated.

The second phase characterizing the violence over time (i.e., the movement from violence to nonviolence) is accompanied by the respondents recognizing a change in the batterer. The nature of this change was described in terms of whether or not the men could (a) control their anger, (b) control their violent behavior, and (c) avoid controlling their partner. If the men had changed in terms of these features, then it was highly likely that the relationship became nonviolent.

In summary, the respondents made sense of the violence and described it to me through the notion of control. In turn, I identified the process of violence by incorporating Mead's conceptualization of the stages of the act and aspects of the self. As was shown, violence is a function of the self, especially the nature of the "Me" that the person has. The "Me" is a function of childhood experiences and the current situation, including how significant others view the self and what they expect. The violent act is an interactive process in which the "I" and "Me" continually alternate and intrude into the violence.

Because longitudinal data were obtained, I was also able to identify the process of violence over time. It was revealed that, over time, violence is primarily carried out to control the woman. The interactive process that results in controlling the woman through violence was placed within the Meadian act.

Though there are some limitations to this study, including having a small sample and interviewing only batterers who are in therapy, the strengths of this research should not be understated. The data that was collected is rich and detailed, comprising over 80 hours of talk. Given that the batterers were in treatment, they were probably more prone to sharing their feelings and thoughts about their violence. Their openness enabled me to pursue sensitive issues that have never been captured before in an in-depth manner. Past researchers have too often neglected the batterer's perspective when explaining why violence arises. I also made a serious endeavor to describe the nature of violence over time. Researchers must keep in mind that violence is a reoccurring phenomenon, and this should be directly incorporated into studies on abuse.

The Men's and Women's Perspectives

One of the unique features of this study is that it incorporates both the man's and woman's perspective in order to fully understand the dynamics of violence. The exculsion of either perspective results in a variety of biases and missing information.

Though the interactionist model explains male violence, the woman's behavior is still relevant in understanding why men are violent. As was shown in Chapter 7, she affects and is affected by her partner's violence. Therefore, the women's behavior should not be ignored when interpreting the model. For example, problematic situations often arise when the *woman* challenges her partner's right to control her. This challenge threatens the man's control, and he may respond violently to regain control, especially if the expectations of the "Me," in the perception stage, are to be violent. The violent expectations are likely to be influenced not only by past experiences and how significant others currently expect the man to behave, but also by the way the woman expects her partner to behave. For example, I showed in Chapter 6 how Jackie's use of violence appeared to influence Henry's response to be violent. Apparently, if a woman views violence as an appropriate response, this may influence a violent response from her partner.

The violence is likely to be repeated in the future, especially if the man does' not suffer negative repercussions for his behavior. The woman has some influence on whether or not the man's violence continues. If the woman indirectly rewards the batterer for behaving violently, the violence is likely to continue in the future. She may inadvertently do this in a number of ways—for example, by submitting to his control after a violent episode, by not holding her partner responsible for the violence but instead blaming herself, by viewing the violence as an appropriate response to the dispute, or by not punishing him by bringing charges against him. The woman's response to the violence significantly affects her partner's future line of behavior.

Given the findings, the men only refer to control when describing their own emotions and behavior with respect to violence, and the women only mention control when describing the men's behavior. That is, the issue of control only takes on meaning for the men and women when trying to make sense out of those who abuse. The women do not discuss the batterers' emotions as a subjective experience in terms of control or violence in the way that the men do. Similarly, the men do not discuss the women's emotions as lived experience and, in fact, make very little reference to how the women feel, suggesting that they have low role-taking ability. Finally, neither the men nor the women discuss the women's behavior in terms of control.

The men and women provided a similar discussion on the instrumental nature of violence. They both indicated that the woman usually challenged the man's right to control and that, over time, the violence was used in order to control the woman. Additionally, when examining a change in the batterers over time, I found that the men and women agreed that a change in the men included behaving nonviolently and avoiding attempts to control the women.

Though there were similarities in the men's and women's perspectives, there were also differences. For example, when examining the view that behavior was both in and out of the batterers' control, the men and women gave different descriptions. The men indicated their violence was in their control by noting that the damage they did could have been worse. When they discussed their behavior as out of control, they would mention how the violence was an impulsive or irrational response. It is the batterers who *directly* felt their behavior was impulsive or knew that they had the capacity to inflict more injury onto the women but stopped short of that. The women could not directly experience their partners' feelings when they behaved violently; they could not experience the impulsivity or sense of possibly hitting harder but holding back. They could only experience the behavior that was enacted.

The women described their partner's behavior as in or out of control by indicating the degree to which the behavior was predictable. If the violence was viewed as unpredictable, it implied that the batterer had no control over his actions. Sometimes they would also actually use the term "out of control" to describe the violent behavior. When they viewed the violence as predictable, this suggested that their partner had some control. In addition, they might mention that their partner knew exactly what he was doing, again implying that he had control over his behavior.

I would argue that the woman's perception of her partner's behavior as unpredictable is similar to the man's perception of his behavior as impulsive. Neither the man or woman is indicating that the man's behavior, in general, is unpredictable: we all want to believe that our behavior, on the whole, is consistent or that we are involved with someone who is fairly consistent. Rather, they are both saying, but in different ways, that sometimes when violence occurs, it is unexpected.

There are other differences between the men's and women's perspectives that should be highlighted. First, though the women discussed incidents in more detail than the men, the men were more likely to discuss elements of control regarding specific incidents. When the women discussed the notion of control, they were more likely to mention it in terms of the violence in general. This suggests that if we want to know how control directly relates to the violent act, the batterer's perspective offers more information than the victim's view. Hence, the batterer's perspective, having been neglected in past research, is directly relevant to understanding the underlying process of violence and control.

In those instances where the men and women provided a detailed discussion of the same violent incidents, their descriptions regarding how control related to the violence was sometimes quite different. For example, as mentioned in Chapter 6, Doug and Wendy had an argument over who was going to buy the toilet paper. The argument resulted in a violent incident. Doug claimed that his violence during the first act of the violent episode was controlled, but in the second act, he carried out the impulse to aggress without control. From Wendy's perspective, however, Doug carried out the impulse to aggress from the moment the incident began. In another example, Frank and Nancy had an argument over the fact that Nancy had bought some cigarettes. Frank claims that, rather than being violent in response to her buying the cigarettes, he controlled the impulse to aggress. However, from Nancy's perspective, it was she, not Frank, who stopped Frank from hitting her.

We must keep in mind that the women may not actually challenge their partner's right to control them. Instead, the men may *perceive* their partner's behavior as threatening. For example, it is difficult to imagine that Wendy was challenging Doug by asking him to buy some toilet paper or that Nancy was challenging Frank by buying cigarettes. Therefore, what may be more relevant in precipitating violence is the men's *interpretation* that their partner's behavior is threatening their control.

These examples suggest that having both perspectives enables us to find out several things. First, while a batterer may take a particular path in the violent act, such as Frank inhibiting the impulse to aggress, it may not be of his own choice but rather a result of the woman's behavior. Second, while a batterer may claim to have taken a particular path or paths in the violent episode (such as Doug's mentioning that he first controlled the impulse to aggress and then carried out the impulse to aggress), having the woman's perspective opens up the possibility that how control operates may be quite different from what the man claims (as in the case of Wendy's suggesting that, from the moment the incident began, Doug carried out the impulse to aggress).

In short, the interactionist model provides an overall understanding of how violence is embedded in the stages of the act and how it relates to self-concept. When we examine particular violent incidents where the men and women disagree on how the violence was carried out or who was responsible for whether or not violence occurred, it is difficult to make any conclusions about how violence relates to control in terms of the interactionist model. However, it should be pointed out that both the man's and the woman's perspective is incorporated in the model, so that if there was a disagreement in describing the relationship between control and violence, either the man's or the woman's perspective could be understood in terms of the model.

As mentioned in Chapter 6, it is not surprising that the women discussed more violent incidents in detail than the men. It is likely that the batterers would suffer more guilt and shame than the victims when discussing the incidents and thus be more likely not to mention them. Moreover, women may be more likely to remember specific incidents simply because they received the violence. The violence was more salient to them, having been directly affected by it. The men may have been more likely to forget specific violent incidents in order to preserve their self-esteem. Indeed, some of the batterers in this study did mention forgetting specific details of incidents or completely forgetting incidents that occurred. Finally, the batterers discussed fewer incidents in detail, perhaps because they were more likely to focus on the "ends" rather than the "means" by which they achieved those ends. What was relevant for the men was not if or how they were violent but rather if and when they were successful in regaining control over their partner.

In keeping with what women recall as opposed to what men recall, I found that the loving stage, which Walker (1979b) indicates is the third stage in the battering cycle, was identifiable, in this study, almost only in the women's accounts. This does not imply that the loving stage does not exist—two men offered evidence that some sort of "making up" did exist after an incident—but rather that it typically appears in the women's accounts. This is in keeping with the fact that Walker found the loving stage to exist based on interviews with abused women. Therefore, not only does the man's violent behavior become salient to the woman, but also his behavior after an incident. It is possible that a batterer may not indicate his loving or apologetic behavior after an incident because this would be admitting both to himself and to the researcher that he was sorry for what he had done. In turn, this sorrow would imply that he was responsible for the injury he inflicted, that it was his fault, and perhaps he does not want to admit this.

Hence, individuals in a violent relationship tend to focus on different things because of their different roles (that is, as the perpetrator or victim of violence). Researchers need to account for these varying roles and examine how this influences interpretations of violence in general and in detailed incidents.

Implications of Research Regarding Control and Violence

Having found that control is the most central, meaningful object in respondent's descriptions of the violence, it follows that there are practical, theoretical, methodological, and more general implications that need to be discussed. First, let me turn to the practical implications of this research. Strategies, such as the creation of abuse centers designed to reduce domestic violence, need to incorporate the notion of control into the program format. Women should be educated about how control operates in a domestic violent situation. More importantly, batterers need to be aware of the control aspects of their violence.

Interestingly, in an effort to reduce domestic violence, therapy-based programs that treat men who batter have focused on the issue of control. For example, Ganley (1982) has published a manual to be used by organizations nationwide that seek to create a male batterers treatment program. In the manual, she notes:

Men who batter are often characterized as having a great need to control situations, people, etc. They usually define this control as being "in charge" of external situations. Rarely do they define control in terms of self-control. When experiencing feelings that they interpret as being out of control, attempts to regain a sense of well-being are usually moves to dominate others through aggression and violence. They do not identify that sometimes the source and often the solution to being out of control is internal rather than external. The treatment approaches described later accept the overwhelming need of the man who batters to be in control, but refocuses the object of that control from others to self. (Ganley, 1982, pp. 31–32)

It appears that the practical experience that officials in male battering programs have accumulated over time through talking with batterers, and the treatment approaches that they have used in response to this interaction, can be based on the theoretical understandings gained from this study. I have found that batterers do feel out of control emotionally and behaviorally and want to control their partner. Yet, it must be reiterated that the men in this study were all in some sort of treatment, whether the male batterers program, individual or couple counseling. Hence, they may have been more likely to focus on control because of their participation in treatment. Future research needs to examine the extent to which control appears with men not in treatment. Nonetheless, male battering program officials who address the issue of control by teaching the batterer how to control his aggression (as opposed to controlling the other), may be helping to effectively reduced violence.

Indeed, a national survey of male battering programs (Pirog-Good & Stets, 1986) found that 96% of administrative officials indicate that a strategy of their program is to develop alternatives to battering in order to teach the men how to control their violence. Examples include time-outs, empathizing with the victim, and tension-reducing exercises. Ganley (1982) discusses the timeout procedure. When a batterer senses his anger building and possibly escalating into battering, he is instructed to immediately leave the situation and engage in some physical activity to reduce his arousal. He should return to the situation only when he feels he is calm and relaxed.

In short, programs that treat male batterers have recognized the control aspects of domestic violence and have attempted to deal with them. Through practical experience with batterers, they have come to understand why batterers are violent, and programs have responded with treatment approaches that help curb and/or stop future violence. Alternative approaches to reducing domestic violence need to incorporate the feature of control into their formats.

In addition to the policy implications of control and violence, there are some theoretical and methodological implications of this research. In Chapter 5, the focus was on the relationship between violence, control, the stages of the act, and the "I" and "Me" in terms of why men are violent. This model examined male violence primarily because the men were the aggressors in this study. However, there is no reason to think that this model could not explain women's violence as well. The processes are likely to be the same, such as the "I" carrying out the impulse to aggress without control unless it is interrupted by the "Me," in which case the violence would be viewed as more controlled. Additionally, for women as well as for men, the "Me" in the perception stage is likely to consist of expectations to be violent or nonviolent.

Though I found that the issue of control often precipitated the use of violence for men, it is possible that women are violent for other reasons. Women may not view a challenge to control as a reason for striking out. Women are less likely than men to be in a position of power and may be less likely to feel threatened. Men, who are more likely than women to have power in our society, are more likely to feel threatened when that power is challenged and thus respond negatively in efforts to maintain their dominance. Future research needs to explore those factors that are likely to influence a woman's use of violence.

Future research might also include examining the extent to which the symbolic interactionist model applies to men who are not in therapy. In this study, respondents consisted only of individuals who were participating in treatment. Although there is no evidence (from other research) that the symbolic interactionist process described here operates differently for men not in treatment, this is not to say that this is impossible. For example, men in treatment may be more likely to check the impulse to aggress than men not in treatment. Additionally, men in treatment may be more likely to experience guilt after a violent incident than nontreated men. Issues such as these need to be explored.

One might argue that control was a central issue in this research because the issue of control was a formal part of the batterer's therapy program. This argument would suggest that the findings are an artifact of what the men were experiencing in therapy. This was not the case, however. The issue of control was not a formal part of any therapy program that the individuals were in. When I ask the batterers what they dealt with in therapy, control was never mentioned. Additionally, when I asked the male battering counselors if control was a formal feature of their treatment program, they said that it was not.

Given the symbolic interactionist model presented in Chapter 4, future researchers need to ask more specific questions in order to better capture the relationship between control, the stages of the act, and relevance of the "I" and "Me." For example, in order to more directly examine how the intrusion of the "Me" in the violent act affects the probability of being violent, it would be useful to ask respondents how they thought others expected the man to act at the time that particular violent acts occurred. In order to clarify how control operates in the manipulation stage, and whether manipulation is more characteristic of carrying out the impulse to aggress or checking the impulse to aggress, it would be helpful to ask how much control the respondent felt he had over the form of violence used during specific incidents. Finally, in order to specify the nature of consummation, it would be useful to ask the respondents how they felt immediately after an incident.

Another issue that needs to be directly addressed is whether early violence is more characteristic of impulsive violence (wanting to strike back) and if later violence is more representative of instrumental violence (wanting to control the woman). One might want to ask what made a batterer stop his violence at the particular point in the incident that he did. If the response entails the notion of having done enough injury, then the violence would be representative of impulsiveness. However, if the response entails having finally realized that the victim had been successfully controlled, then the violence would be more representative of instrumentality.

If impulsive violence is more representative of early rather than later battering, then the extent to which this transformation exists needs to be captured. A way to do this would be to compare respondents who have been involved in a violent relationship for a long time with those who have just entered a violent relationship. Moreover, it would be useful to closely follow those individuals who have just entered a violent relationship to see whether the violence is transformed, over time, to instrumentality.

Still another issue that should be further explored is when violence occurs in a relationship. Evidence from this study revealed that violence was most likely to occur and reoccur after the relationship had been established as serious. A relationship was considered serious if the individuals spent a lot of time with each other, including sexual intimacy, cohabitation, or marriage. Violence was not likely to arise until this point. The fact that violence occurs in serious relationships supports other research (Stets & Pirog-Good, 1987). What may be happening is that once a relationship becomes defined as serious, the woman becomes viewed as the man's property and thus someone over whom he has control. Early battering has the unintended consequences of controlling the woman. However, control becomes more relevant as the serious relationship becomes more committed and intimate, and violence is used with the intent of controlling the woman.

Despite evidence that violence is more likely to occur in long-term relationships, it is possible that if the man is violent to the woman in early dating, a relationship may not develop in the first place. It may be easier for a woman to leave her dating partner early in the relationship if she does not have much invested in the relationship. In contrast, a woman in a serious relationship may find it harder to leave her partner simply because her investment is greater.

Finally, there are more general implications to this research on control and violence in relationships. One might speculate on the degree to which control operates in other violent relationships. Recall that in this study, the sample of respondents were adults who were either in a cohabitating or marital relationship. Violence in college dating relationships may occur due to conflict over control. Indeed, recent research on courtship violence is consistent with this theoretical notion (Stets & Pirog-Good, 1987). To extend the relevance of control to other violent relationships, child abuse in many families may be based on parents seeking to control their children's behavior and the children's attempt to resist. Sibling or elderly abuse may occur because one individual attempts to control the behavior of the other. Future research needs to explore the possible connection between control and violence.

If we extend the analysis of control to other interactions, it is possible that control influences marital separation and/or divorce. Conflict may arise over who has control over financial, household, or entertainment matters. Instead of having arguments that result in violence, these individuals may instead walk away from the conflict, perhaps leaving the issue unresolved. Over time, this conflict and lack of working out problems over who has control in particular areas (or agreeing to share in the control) may eventually create a state wherein one or both individuals see no other recourse than to separate or sever the relationship.

The issue of control may also be relevant when problems arise in friendships. Friendships between children, teenagers, and adults may disintegrate as the issue of control increasingly takes precedence between friends. One may not like or even permit another to think or behave in a particular fashion and may attempt to exert power over the other.

To a large degree, violence against women continues to exist because our society still gives the positions of power largely to men. Men maintain dominance and are given the right to control others in societal institutions because men are the executives in corporations and industries. Men earn more money than women in the labor market, and more money is associated with more power. Given that men still have this power, they will continue to defend their positions and feel that they should be in control. The moment that they perceive a threat to their control, they will use aggression (a behavior that they have learned is connected to masculinity) to defend themselves.

What if women were given equal power in society? One result might be that, having the resources to survive on their own, they would be more apt to leave the abusive relationship. Perhaps only when women assume more positions of power will they come to acknowledge the injustice that they are experiencing in their personal lives and act in a manner that protects themselves and their children.

Future Concerns for Symbolic Interactionists

The objectification of control in interaction is a relatively unexplored area among symbolic interactionists. This research suggests that the notion of control may be very important when trying to understand the dynamics of interaction, and that symbolic interactionists need to attend to it more closely. Moreover, as control is a process, interactionists need to examine how processes become objects in interaction.

Though it is important that symbolic interactionists focus on the notion of control in violent relationships, there are other features of violent relationships that also need to be explored. These features may be relevant toward understanding domestic violence in specific and conflict situations in general. Among these features are an examination of identity, self-esteem, and role-taking ability. Let me briefly address their possible relevance.

According to Stryker (1980) one's identity is "'part' of the self, internalized positional designations . . . thus, a woman may have identities as physician, wife, mother, child, tennis player, Democrat, etc., which taken together comprise the self" (p. 60). Some identities are more salient than others. Because one may have several identities, an actor may invoke a particular identity in a situation that may not be the same identity the other expects the actor to play out. It is possible that this causes conflict and that this conflict leads to violence. For example, on a particular night, a woman may invoke her identity of "wage earner." Her partner may expect her to play out the "mother" identity. Conflict may arise when the woman attempts to complete paperwork she has brought home from the office and her partner expects her to tend to the children. The man may respond violently to this conflict.

In addition, it is important to examine the relationship between identities and the nature of the "Me" in a violent episode. It is possible that the nature of the "Me" (and thus its influence on the violent act) is directly related to the type of identity one claims at the time violence arises. Particular identities have particular "Me's." Moreover, as a situation will influence the type of identity one will call up, the situation may also influence the "Me" and thus, indirectly, affect the violence.

Self-esteem refers to feelings about the value of the self. A low self-esteem is characteristic of lack of self-respect and a feeling of unworthiness, and a high self-esteem results in feelings of self-respect and worthiness (Rosenberg, 1979). One who has a low self-esteem concentrates on the positive qualities of others and desires to be like them. This naturally leads to a derogation of the self because individuals with low self-esteem come to imagine a negative appearance by comparing themselves to the favorable qualities of others. This negativity may explain why some men are violent to women. The man with low self-esteem may seek to defend himself against a negative appearance by attacking his mate. Women in violent relationships may also have low self-esteem. They may feel that they deserve the violence and are not worthy of anything better than that.

Finally, the symbolic interactionist concept of role-taking may help in understanding violence. Role-taking is the process of imaginatively adopting another's roles (their expected behavior patterns) or perspective in interaction (Turner, 1969). It is taking the point of view of the other in order to (a) project how the other will behave, and (b) respond to the actor's conduct. Interactant's inability at role-taking may contribute to the occurrence of domestic violence. It may be that neglecting the perspective of the other leads to conflict and hence violence. Partners may be inaccurate in the anticipation of each other's responses, which may contribute to the response of violence.

Summary

This research has attempted to better understand and conceptualize domestic violence by collecting qualitative data and employing the symbolic interactionist framework. Domestic violence has been viewed as embedded in a stream of on-going, face-to-face interaction. By incorporating both the men's and women's perspectives, I have found that control is a central theme in respondents' descriptions of the violence.

Using a longitudinal framework, I have looked at both the emergence of violence and the movement to nonviolence. It is clear that future research must move away from interviews at one point in time in domestic violence research and examine the longitudinal nature of the violence. We need to be particularly sensitive to changes on an individual and interactive level. We must take seriously the fact that violence does not occur at one point in time. Once it occurs, it reoccurs. This reoccurrence must be incorporated into studies in order to account for the full expression of violence in a relationship.

It should be pointed out that violence against women must be understood not only in the context of the interactive unit in which it is embedded but also in the wider society that generally has supported violence directed at women. There is nothing new about men controlling women through violence. There is also nothing new about women challenging men's right to control them. What is new is that men's traditional rights are no longer viewed as acceptable. Thus, their use of violence against women has come under attack. Feminists have made us aware of the unfair practice of men dominating women. As a result, men and women are learning that it is not a male's right to control a woman, especially when that control takes the form of violence. Indeed, when men begin to learn this, they are no longer violent to their partners, as revealed in this study.

It is interesting that the men and women in this study discussed violence, over time, in terms of controlling the women. Describing the violence in this manner suggests that challenging a male's entitlement to domination in social institutions in the wider society has carried over to challenging their power and control in intimate, face-to-face interaction. As women and men have come to realize that sexism and discrimination in the social structure is a direct result of men's desire to be in control, they have also come to see that how women are treated on a more personal and intimate level is, again, a direct result of men's desire to control. Hence, what occurs on a macro level is reflected on a micro level.

Appendix 1
Data on Couples Over Time (1985)

Interviews

Couple	Respondents	Group Participation	T1	T2	T3	T4
1	Ronald	0 months	1/10	8/13	9/10	10/18
	Kathy		1/16	8/7	9/11	10/9
2	Henry	0 months	3/21	—	—	—
	Jackie		6/13	—	—	—
3	Fred	$1\frac{1}{2}$ months	5/20	8/20	—	—
	Ann		5/30	9/12	10/9	11/5
4	Mike	3 months	6/6	8/20	9/24	10/24
	Kay		6/17	8/19	9/15	10/15
5	Larry	0 months	6/4	8/22	9/18	10/16
	Terri		6/14	8/16	9/17	10/17
6	Doug	3 months	6/3	8/21	9/17	10/19
	Wendy		6/5	8/24	10/11	11/18
7	Kevin	0 months	6/14	9/4	10/2	11/11
	Lisa		6/19	8/21	9/24	10/22
8	Bill	3 months	7/16	8/21	9/19	10/16
	Jane		—	—	—	—
9	Frank	3 months	7/17	8/23	9/27	10/25
	Nancy		7/18	9/2	9/30	10/28

Note. T1 = initial interview; T2 = second interview; T3 = third interview; T4 = final interview.

Appendix 2A
Letter to Male Participants

TO: MALE PARTICIPANT   DATE: January, 1985

FROM: Jan E. Stets

I am studying the problem of domestic violence in order to obtain a better understanding of why it happens. In order to understand why one person might hurt another in a relationship, it is important to know how each partner views the relationship. Many researchers, while focusing on the woman's perspective, have neglected the man's point of view. I am interested in EACH PARTNER'S interpretation of their situation since this influences why they behave as they do.

With your cooperation, I will conduct the research in the following way. I will conduct a series of in-depth tape recorded interviews with you. I will interview you before you enter the program soon after you have met with John Jones and/or Sam Williams. Once you begin the program, I will interview you every month for three months. After you have left the program, I will meet with you for one or more follow-ups.

I want to assure you of several things before you begin participation in this project. First, you can refuse to answer any questions I ask you in the interviews which are too stressful for you to deal with. Second, I believe there are no right or wrong answers to any of the questions. As a researcher, I will remain value-neutral to your responses. Third, your answers will remain confidential and anonymous such that any findings that result from this research will not be traced back to what you might have said. Attached is an informed consent form that I would like you to read and sign. If you have any questions concerning this research, please feel free to call me. I look forward to meeting you.

Sincerely,

Jan E. Stets

Appendix 2B
Informed Consent Form to
Male Participants

I, _____, have agreed to participate in a research project on domestic violence. I understand that participation in this research requires that I participate in in-depth tape recorded interviews with Jan E. Stets upon program entrance, then every month for three months, and after program completion, for one or more follow-ups. I am aware that: 1) if any questions are too stressful for me, I do not have to answer them, and 2) my answers will remain confidential and anonymous. I have the freedom to withdraw this consent and not participate in this research at any time even after initial participation and will not suffer any negative consequences from doing so.

IF YOU HAVE ANY QUESTION BEFORE SIGNING, PLEASE CONTACT THE RESEARCHER.

_____
(date)

_____
(signature)

Appendix 3A
Letter to Female Participants

TO: FEMALE PARTICIPANT   DATE: January, 1985

FROM: Jan E. Stets

I am conducting a research project concerning the problem of domestic violence in order to obtain a better understanding of why it happens. In order to understand why one person might hurt another in a relationship, it is important to know how each partner views the relationship. Many researchers, while focusing on the woman's perspective, have neglected the man's point of view. I am interested in EACH PARTNER'S interpretation of their situation since this influences why they behave as they do.

With your cooperation, I will conduct the research with you in the following way. I will conduct an in-depth, tape recorded interview with you before your partner enters the male batterers program. Once he begins the program, I will interview you every month for three months. After he has left the program, I will meet with you for one or more follow-ups.

I want to assure you of several things before you begin participation in this project. First, you can refuse to answer any questions I ask you in the interviews which are too stressful for you to deal with. Second, I believe there are no right or wrong answers to any of the questions. As a researcher, I will remain value-neutral to your responses. Third, your answers will remain confidential and anonymous such that any findings that result from this research will not be traced back to what you might have said. Attached is an informed consent form that I would like you to read and sign. If you have any questions concerning this research, please feel free to call me. I look forward to meeting you.

Sincerely,

Jan E. Stets

Appendix 3B
Informed Consent Form to
Female Participants

I, _____, have agreed to participate in a research project on domestic violence. I understand that participation in this research requires that I participate in in-depth tape recorded interviews with Jan E. Stets upon my partners entrance into the male batterers program, then every month for three months, and after he completes the program, for one or more follow-ups. I am aware that: 1) if any questions are too stressful for me, I do not have to answer them and 2) my answers will remain confidential and anonymous. I have the freedom to withdraw this consent and not participate in this research at any time even after initial participation and will not suffer any negative consequences from doing so.

IF YOU HAVE ANY QUESTIONS BEFORE SIGNING, PLEASE CONTACT THE RESEARCHER.

_____
(date)

_____
(signature)

Appendix 4
Interview Approach

The first step in the interview procedure entailed creating a series of questions intended to uncover facts, attitudes, and feelings about the respondents' past and present experiences that I thought would be relevant to understanding battering. I organized these questions into topics and subtopics and arranged them in a logical order (see Appendix 5). The interview guide, which was brought to initial interviews, served as a reminder of the topics and subtopics that were to be covered.

The interview introduction reviewed issues of sponsorship, purpose of the research, the selection procedure, anonymity of respondent's interviews, and the purpose of taping (Gorden, 1980). I introduced myself as a sociology graduate student who was interested in understanding battering both from the man's and woman's perspective. I indicated that they were selected because the men had contacted the shelter and expressed an interest in the battering program. I stressed confidentiality and indicated that all names and places would be changed to protect the individual respondent's identity. Taping was explained in terms of how it would enable me to obtain exactly what was said.

I decided to start with respondents' pasts (their childhoods) and move to the present. I felt that the movement from past to present would be the easiest cognitive route for them. Moreover, this background information would facilitate a better and more complete understanding of the man's current abusive behavior and the woman's victimization. In addition to obtaining background information on the respondents, the interview guide indicates that the dynamics of the violence was addressed. Understanding the dynamics of violence included considering the source and form of violent incidents and exploring participants' reactions and feelings to violent incidents. Such features were incorporated into the interviews. This interview approach, which moves from the respondent's past to present life experiences and which focuses on the dynamics of violent relationships, supports the approach used by Dobash and Dobash (1979) in their interviews with 109 battered women.

The interview style was formal, semi-structured, open-ended, in-depth, and audiotaped. It was formal because the respondents and I agreed to meet with each other for the purpose of an interview as opposed to an unplanned, naturally occurring meeting. Although my questions and their ordering made explicit what I wanted to cover and when I wanted to cover them, an unstructured approach was still utilized. I wanted to allow myself the freedom to attempt alternative wordings for the same question or questions and be open to shifting the order of subtopics. As my purpose in the interviews was to explore and discover different aspects of abuse, flexibility was needed.

The questions were open-ended as opposed to providing the respondents with a set of fixed responses from which to choose. I did not know, exactly, what the possible range of responses was that one might elicit. The open-ended technique allowed respondents to speak freely and in their own words. This aided in putting the respondent at ease when discussing such sensitive topics as their use or experience of violence. Moreover, the open-ended approach facilitated pursuing additional issues that were not originally planned but had the possibility of being relevant.

An in-depth approach was used because I not only wanted information about events, but also the respondents' reflections on those events. This included their attitudes, feelings, or any other subjective orientation on their experiences. Finally, the interviews were tape recorded. The interview topic and approach met the prerequisites for using a tape recorder:

> The more complex the information, the less the method should depend upon the interviewer's memory. The more rapid the flow of relevant information, the less we should depend upon taking longhand notes. The more we wish to explore for unanticipated types of responses and the less sure we are of what categories of information are relevant to the problem, the more we should use a tape recorder, which omits nothing and allows the relevance of the responses to be decided later . . . The less topic control is used, and the less the sequences of topics is controlled, the more important it is for the interviewer to be relieved of verbatim reporting in longhand and allowed to devote more attention to probe notes. The more important it is for the interviewer to devote full attention to the respondent to obtain optimal interpersonal relations, the more important it is to use the tape recorder. (Gorden, 1980, pp. 224–225)

Tape recording the interviews allowed me the opportunity to adopt a more conversational style and concentrate on the discussion rather than be preoccupied with notetaking. This provided a more relaxed atmosphere for the respondent.

I became sensitive to those features that facilitate and inhibit an interview (Gorden, 1980). For example, giving the respondent recognition, by praising him or her for cooperating in the research, could have had a positive effect on the interviews. On the other hand, threatening the person's ego may have resulted in dishonest answers from the respondent.

Topic controls were used (Gorden, 1980). For instance, a silent response on my part to respondents' answers enabled them to continue their train of thought in a direction that made most sense to them. Another topic control, an immediate clarification, helped establish the meaning of a respondent's state of talk.

Gorden (1980) indicates that a "more neutral ground should be used for the interview, if possible" (p. 201). He argues that a neutral place minimizes biases that may enter the interview. For example, if the interview is conducted in the interviewer's home, the respondent may feel uncomfortable because of the unfamiliar environment. This may influence respondents not to reveal what they would if the setting were neutral. The respondent may also experience a higher degree of chronological confusion or ego threat.

I initially decided that a neutral place for my interviews would be an office in the administrative suite at a midwestern shelter for abused women. It would suffice in eliminating distractions and some bias. I used the location for my first interviews with Ronald, Kathy, Henry, and Fred. After that, however, I began to have problems with obtaining the room for interviews. Though the shelter director would agree to leave me a key to the door, she frequently forgot. As a result, I had to move several of my initial interviews, at the last minute, to different locations. I decided to move them to an office on a nearby university campus. When I realized that last-minute changes in my interview location would be inconvenient for many of my subjects if such a situation continued, I decided to relocate all of my interviews to this office on campus because I was always assured of access to the room. When respondents felt that my location was an inconvenient place for them to meet at a particular time, I adjusted to their needs. For example, I conducted my second interview with Lisa in a city park because Kevin was out of town for several weeks and she needed to watch her children at the same time she met with me. She suggested the locale and I agreed.

Gorden (1980) also notes that it is best to select a time of day for an interview in which the respondent has "fewest competing time demand" (p. 205). I interviewed most of the respondents in the early evening. I suspected that a daytime appointment would probably conflict with job or child care responsibilities and a mid- to late evening appointment might not provide an alert respondent. If a respondent wanted to meet in the early morning or afternoon, I agreed.

Before each session, I went early to the room to review what I would be covering in the interview. I set up the tape recorder and made sure it was working properly and was relatively unobtrusive. If a respondent did not show up, I waited for approximately 15 minutes beyond the prearranged time and then called to see what had happened. I thought about calling respondents the day before their scheduled interview to remind them of our appointment. This may have prevented the problem of some of my subjects forgetting the interview and not showing up. I would then have to reschedule with them. I decided not to call every subject beforehand, but if

I knew a particular individual had a tendency to forget our interview, I would call as a reminder. This never caused a problem and, in fact, the respondent seemed to appreciate the reminder.

Each interview lasted for an average of about an hour and a half. Therefore, the total amount of time I spent talking with the majority of the subjects about their violent relationships ranged from four to six hours. Throughout the interviews, I sometimes jotted down notes regarding something that the respondent said that I thought would be an important issue to pursue a bit further. This strategy enabled respondents to complete their train of thought without interruption. We could then continue the interview by covering the necessary points until it was appropriate to bring up further issues from my notes.

After each interview, I wrote a brief summary of what was discussed in the interview and my general feelings regarding the interview and respondent. The interview guide in Appendix 6 outlines those issues that were discussed beyond the initial interview. These items had the possibility of changing over time.

In reviewing the first interview with each respondent after it was conducted and transcribed, some problems arose. Sometimes I needed clarification of a particular issue a respondent had discussed, and at other times, I felt it necessary to further explore an attitude or feeling that a respondent had not elaborated on. These issues were addressed at the beginning of the next interview with the respondents. Once this was completed, we discussed what had developed since the last time we talked. This approach was repeated in the third and fourth interviews.

Questions regarding a prior interview varied according to the individual. For example, some individuals in the initial interview would be explicit about what happened prior to an incident and how each reacted after the violence. Others might gloss over precipitating and subsequent events of a violent incident and share what they were feeling at the time: for example, guilt over hitting another or fear of the violence. Therefore, the information that could be obtained in the initial interview might be very different depending on what the respondents shared. As my endeavor in the initial session was to obtain background information on the respondents and the history of the violence, I withheld asking a lot of clarification questions. On the one hand, I was not sure how much detail I wanted. On the other hand, it was my first interview with the respondents, and I felt that I needed some time to get to know them and build some trust. It was in the second interview that I felt comfortable enough to obtain more detail about what the respondents had said. For those who had provided detail on precipitating and subsequent events, I pursued how they felt at that time. For those who had glossed over prior and subsequent events, I tried to get some detail about what they thought caused the violence and how they and their partner reacted following the violence.

In the second, third, and fourth interviews with the respondents, I felt comfortable enough to get immediate clarification and perhaps more detail on what they were saying. When I reviewed the transcripts after the interview and decided that I needed more information, I would ask for it in the next interview. For example, some individuals might indicate, in the second interview, that they would talk after a violent incident. In the interview, I would ask them when and what they talked about. For those who did not indicate that they talked after an incident, I would ask them if they did, when, and what they talked about. After beginning to explore the aspect of communication, I began to realize that this might be a relevant feature of the interaction. Therefore, in the third interview, I asked respondents the degree to which communication occurred in early as opposed to later violence in the relationship and the nature of the communication.

Appendix 5
Interview Guide

Introduction: Cover

a. Sponsorship
b. Purpose of interview
c. Selection process
d. Confidentiality
e. Taping
f. Note-taking

General information on subject's background

a. Parent's occupation
b. Relationship with parents and siblings; relationship between parents
c. Degree to which subject experienced and/or witnessed violence when young

Youth

a. Dating relationships
b. Use and/or experience of violence

Current Relationship

a. History and growth of relationship
b. Attitude and feelings on relationshp
c. Arguments—source and frequency
d. Expectations

Violence

a. First incident as a reference to begin with—source and form
b. History of violent incidents that followed—source and form
c. Reactions of self and other after incidents occurred including feelings and behavior
d. General source and feelings about why it happens

Network of others

a. Children—relationship with them; do they hit them; what do children do when spousal violence occurs
b. Degree to which there is social support from family and friends

Future

a. Hopes and aims for the future with regard to the relationship and violence
b. General feelings about self and what has happend

Appendix 6
Interview Guide Over Time

Review
a. Issues from prior interview that were not clear

Current Relationship
a. Attitudes and feelings on relationshp
b. Arguments—source and frequency
c. Communication

Violence
a. Frequency and form
b. Reactions (feelings and behavior) after violent incidents
c. Feelings about why it happened

Attitudes
a. Feelings about self and other
b. Changes in self and other

Counseling
a. Form and frequency of counseling
b. What is discussed

Future
a. Hopes and aims for the future with regard to the relationship and violence
b. Goals

Appendix 7
Coding Procedure

Codes were developed in the following way. First, I obtained one interview of all the subjects from different points in time. Then, while reading the interview content, I placed a topic name (code) beside each excerpt of the interview to indicate the theme of what was being discussed. The interview content was thus broken down into themes. Approximately 55 codes were generated.

I used the 55 codes to continue coding more interviews but then realized that (a) the codes needed to be explicitly defined, and (b) some excerpts of the interviews required multiple codes. One theme could not capture the discussion of multiple issues. Then, I returned to the first set of interviews that had been coded, applied multiple codes where necessary, and defined each code. As a result, additions and deletions were made to the original list of 55 codes. The final list included approximately 45 codes. Below is an interview excerpt from my first session with Kathy to illustrate this procedure.

THINGS/VIOLENCE, NEW MATE, FORM OF VIOLENCE, INCIDENT
Finally, after a couple of days he told me that, and that he wanted to have other relationships. So, both of us started having other relationships. And I got involved with somebody and he started sleeping around. Then, the other time when he hit me was when I was talking about Mike, which is the man I moved in with for awhile. I was only talking about it, but like he would ask me something and then I made some statement, and he would ask me about Mike so I told him, and then he would get mad at me for telling him. And so, this one time, we were at Mark and Joan's again, and he mentioned something, I don't remember what it was now or what the exact words were. But that was the time when I think he kicked me in the chest, and I think he came over and held my shoulders and slammed my head against the floor. And that was the one time he actually hurt me. All the other times it didn't hurt, but like my jaw was sore.

When I first coded this excerpt, I attached the code THINGS/ VIOLENCE to the discussion. I defined this code as an instance where respondents indicated, either directly or indirectly, the source of a specific violent incident or the violence in general. The cause of the violence

(THINGS LEADING TO VIOLENCE) might be conflict over finances, pressures at work, or unmet expectations regarding duties and obligations at home. Kathy's excerpt implies that Ronald's jealousy was the source of at least one violent incident.

Kathy is identifying much more than what leads to violence, however. She is also indicating that she started dating someone else (NEW MATE), that a violent incident had occurred at about this time (INCIDENT), and the type of violence Ronald used (FORM OF VIOLENCE). I defined a NEW MATE as another individual (other than one's partner) that either the respondent was dating or living with whether or not the couple was currently cohabitating, married, or not seeing each other. Therefore, a new mate might indicate an extramarital affair, additional dating relationship, or new dating relationship that either the respondent had experienced or was currently experiencing since the beginning of the couple's relationship. An INCIDENT was an episode that inflicted physical pain or injury or otherwise mistreated the woman in the relationship. Finally, the FORM OF VIOLENCE represented the type of physical force that was used on the woman. Because these three codes also described elements of Kathy's excerpt, I added them to the code, THINGS/VIOLENCE.

When the coding was finished, the codes were typed into all the transcribed interview computer files. Then, using a FORTRAN program, all the excerpts of a particular code were pulled from all the files and placed in a single file. Thus, all examples of each code appear together in one file. When I wanted to examine the features of a particular code, I called up the file that had all the interview excerpts with that specific code attached to it.

Appendix 8A
Demographic Characteristics of Respondents

Demographic Characteristics	Couples									
	1		2		3		4		5	
	Ron	Kathy	Henry	Jackie	Fred	Ann	Mike	Kay	Larry	Terri
Age										
21–25			X			X				X
26–30	X	X		X	X		X	X	X	
31–35										
Race										
White	X	X	X	X	X	X	X	X	X	X
Black										
Marital status										
Never married	X	X	X						X	X
Married					X	X				
Separated							X	X		
Divorced				X						
Religion										
None	X			X					X	X
Protestant										
Catholic			X							
Jewish		X								
Other					X	X	X	X		

Note. $N = 18$.

	Couples						
	6		7		8		9
Doug	Wendy	Kevin	Lisa	Bill	Jane	Frank	Nancy
	X				X		X
X		X	X	X		X	
X	X	X	X		X		X
				X		X	
	X			X	X		
		X	X				
X						X	X
					X	X	X
		X	X	X			
X	X						

Appendix 8B
Demographic Characteristics of Respondents

Demographic Characteristics	Couples									
	1		2		3		4		5	
	Ron	Kathy	Henry	Jackie	Fred	Ann	Mike	Kay	Larry	Terri
Education										
High school diploma					X	X				
Some college							X		X	
College degree	X	X						X		X
Graduate school			X	X						
Employment										
Full time	X			X				X	X	
Part time		X	X				X			X
Unemployed					X	X				
Joint income										
> $5,999							X	X		
$6,000–9,999					X	X				
$10,000–13,999	X	X	X	X						
$14,000–17,999									X	X
$18,000–21,999										
$22,000–25,999										
$26,000–29,999										
$30,000–33,999										
$34,000 +										

Note. $N = 18$.

Couples							
6		7		8		9	
Doug	Wendy	Kevin	Lisa	Bill	Jane	Frank	Nancy
				X			X
X	X				X		
			X				
		X				X	
		X				X	
	X			X	X		
X			X				X
				X	X		
X	X					X	X
		X	X				

Appendix 9
Treatment Methods for Respondents Over Time (1985)

Counseling methods

Respondent	Individual	Group	Group (other)	Couple	Marital
Ronald	T2				
Kathy					
Henry				T1	
Jackie				T1	
Fred		T1–T2			
Ann					
Mike	T1–T4	T1–T4			T3
Kay	T1–T2				T3
Larry	T1–T4		T1–T4	T2–T4	
Terri	T4		T1	T2–T4	
Doug	T1–T4	T1–T4	T1–T4		
Wendy			T1–T4		
Kevin					T2
Lisa					T2
Bill		T1–T4	T1–T4		
Jane					
Frank		T1– T4			
Nancy					

Note. Group (other) = participation in a women's group, AA, or AlAnon. T1 = initial interview; T2 = second interview; T3 = third interview; T4 = final interview.

Appendix 10
The Absence of Control

Doug discussed an incident that occurred. He had asked his partner Wendy to go to an Alcoholics Anonymous meeting. Wendy had agreed, and Doug thought she interpreted it as a date. When they arrived there, Wendy expected Doug to go in with her. When he refused, she refused to go in as well. The discussion escalated into an argument, and Doug eventually hit Wendy. He describes what happened in this way:

"You need to go to this. Will you go to it?" She says, "Yeah, I'll go to it." She looks at it like I ask her to go to a meeting with me. Like it's a date. Like she'll go with me as a date, but she won't go because she needs to go. She goes because Doug wants me to be with him . . . And it's just like, I want her to go because she needs it. And when we got there . . . This was about a month ago. Sunday evening, 6 o'clock or something. And we got up there, and I said, "You go up there, I'll hold the baby." And I said, "I'll stay here." "Go on up and go to the meeting, and I'll just sit out here." "Well I thought we were going to go to the meeting." Puts this we shit in there. "I ain't doing nothing. Why don't you go to the meeting?" She wouldn't go. "Well I don't want to go if you don't want to go." "Will you get your ass up in that meeting." I was having a hard time. I was trying to impress upon her. I said, "You're going to that meeting if I got to drag your ass up there. You're going to that meeting. Get your ass up there." And she says, "Oh, you're just kidding with me. You're not serious." And I said, "I'm serious, bitch. Get your ass up there." "Oh, you're just kidding me, Doug." And I said, "I'm not kidding you, goddammit, get up there." "Oh, you're just kidding me." So I said, "If I was kidding you, I wouldn't want to drag your ass up those stairs." "Oh, you're just teasing me." She's in a fucking fantasy. "I'm serious, now get up there." And I did it. I finally, I worked myself up. I was just real angry, and she wouldn't go, and I couldn't stand the way the situation was any more, just living like that, and she needed help, and I wanted her to get some goddam help. So I was going to drag her ass up there. And I didn't give a shit. I just got to this point where my mind just clicked and fuck this, I don't care. She will go up these stairs. And she started screaming or something, and I think I backhanded her or smacked her or something. Cause I was going to smack her upside the head like that, and then she started getting smart-alecky with me and I just slapped her up the other side of the head and "Sit down and stay there. And next time, I'm going to break your fucking nose. Don't be a smart ass." She cooled out some. Some neighbor guy or something saw it and came, and I said "Call 'em." And he did, and the police came, and at this point, we're deciding that she's going to leave me there or something. And I told her, "Head on over to the apartment and give me my things before you leave." The cops came and "What's going on?" And the neighbors are just hanging out there watching and all this shit. And she starts thinking, "Well, I don't want to leave you by yourself without a ride home." And the cops are, "What do you think, he's going to hurt you? You think you'll be all right?" It wound up, we both went to the AA meeting or some shit down the road.

Doug did not make any direct or indirect reference to whether he was in or out of control when he was violent. Because this does not provide evidence on how control might be related to violence, it is not included in the analysis.

Appendix 11
Applying the Model to Violence Toward Men

Ronald's incident with his friend provides an example of how the expectations of the "Me" to be nonviolent (2 in Figure 5.1) may be related to carrying out the impulse to aggress (Path F). Before illustrating this, a preliminary remark is necessary. A violent incident may have more than one act. For example, I presented earlier an excerpt from my initial interview with Kathy of a detailed violent incident. This incident has two acts. The first act begins with their argument over Ronald's friends and ends with Kathy going into her room and crying. The second act begins with Ronald entering Kathy's room and ends with Kathy crying again. The second act does not necessarily have to be another violent occurrence, as will be seen in the incident that Ronald describes. What is clear, however, is that the event that ends one act may be a cue for an additional act. The episode that Ronald describes is made up of two acts. Each will be discussed. First, let me discuss the expectations of the "Me."

In my first interview with Ronald, he indicated that his father often smacked him on the side of the head. He also mentioned that he used to break a lot of things around the house when he was young. Despite the fact that he experienced violence, Ronald noted that he never saw his father hit his mother. In our second interview, Ronald was seeing a therapist. He said:

My dad used to hit me on the head all the time, and I used to break windows at home so we just dealt with that whole thing. It seems like it must be somewhat related. I learned really early that hitting is a legitimate form of communication to the point where I never used to say my dad beat me.

In this interview and in interviews that followed, it appeared that Ronald's "Me" was changing to the point that he was concentrating on ways in which to control his violent tendency. Part of this was a result of his participation in individual counseling, which is referred to in the excerpts below. The excerpts highlight the changing "Me":

And it gave me the handle that I need, and where I'm at now is that I'm still monitoring it on my own, and when I feel that I'm in the position that I need it to be monitored again, I've got someone more directly to go back to . . . I have to hedge a little bit. I have it under control to the extent if it comes unglued again, I know how to get it back in line. But I'm not guaranteeing. . . But I feel in control of it enough to be able to help people and say, "Sure I was an alcoholic, but now I don't drink. I beat someone, but I've got it in control, and this is what I've done, and everything happens this is who I call, and this is what I do. And you can take your chance or not."

Through individual counseling, he was acquiring a new set of expectations, that is, to control his violence.

Ronald was on vacation last summer visiting some friends. During his stay, he got into an argument with one friend and, in the following statement, describes what happened:

He said, "Don't come back to New Jersey." He started screaming at me. And I said, "Fuck you." And I kicked at his flower pots that he had in his hand. And then I realized, "Oh shit, he just made me lose my temper again. After all this work I've done."

Ronald indicates that his violent response—kicking the flower pot out of his friend's hand—was out of control. He lost his temper. Therefore, one can assume that he carried out the impulse to aggress (Path *F* in Figure 5.1). Ronald felt bad about this response, perhaps feeling that he failed himself. This is represented in his remarks, "After all this work I've done." He had been working on controlling his violence. Therefore, the first part of the incident (the first act) was perceived by Ronald as being out of control.

The second part of the incident (the second act) began after Ronald lost his temper:

So I just went and packed up the car, and I was just going to come home right that night. And I went out of the door, and I said goodbye, and he gave me this real sad look and so I said, "Look, do you want to talk about it or not?" And he said, "Yes." So went went and talked about it. And then he told me all this shit about him and Alice. All the head trips . . . So, the bad thing that happened was he made me lose my temper. Not he made me lose my temper. Bad language. The bad thing that happened was how I lost my temper. But the good thing that happened was for me that I packed up and was ready to leave, but then I went back to talk to him and said, "Look. What's it going to be?" And then when he started giving me more shit about what I was doing, that I kept putting it back on him and saying that I wasn't doing anything. It was the situation that was wrong. What he finally came out and said was that he was never trying to blame me. He was always trying to blame the situation, and I told him that his language really sucked. Ha. So, I was very in control. I quickly realized what had gone wrong and was able to deal with it, accordingly.

Ronald indicated that he was about to leave and return home but then decided to talk to his friend about what had happened. When Ronald says that he was "very in control," it appears that he is suggesting that the discussion could have led to violence again but that he controlled himself, thus inhibiting the impulse to aggress (Path *A* in Figure 5.1).

References

Athens, L.H. (1977). Violent crime: A symbolic interactionist study. *Journal of Symbolic Interaction*, *1*, 56–70.

Athens, L.H. (1980). *Violent criminal acts and actors: A symbolic interactionist study*. Boston: Routledge and Kegan Paul.

Athens L.H. (1986). Types of violent persons: Toward the development of a symbolic interactionist theory of violent criminal behavior. *Studies in Symbolic Interaction*, *7*, 367–390.

Averill, J.R. (1976). Emotion and anxiety: Sociocultural, biological, and psychological determinants. In M. Zuckerman & C.D. Spielberger (Eds.). *Emotions and Anxiety: New Concepts, Methods, and Applications* (pp. 87–130). Hillsdale, NJ: Lawrence Erlbaum Associates.

Averill, J.R. (1980). A constructionist view of emotion. In R. Plutchik & H. Kellerman (Eds.). *Emotion: Theory, research, and experience* (pp. 305–309). New York: Academic Press.

Bagarozzi, D.A., & Giddings C.W. (1983). Conjugal violence: A critical review of current research and clinical practices. *The American Journal of Family Therapy*, *11*, 3–15.

Bandura, A., Ross D., & Ross S.A. (1961). Transmission of aggression through imitation of aggressive models. *Journal of Abnormal and Social Psychology*, *63*, 575–582.

Berkowitz, L. (1983). The goals of aggression. In D. Finkelhor et al. (Eds.). *The dark side of families: Current family violence research* (pp. 166–181). Beverly Hills: Sage Publications.

Blumer, H. (1969). *Symbolic interaction: Perspective and method*. Englewood Cliffs, NJ: Prentice-Hall.

Bolton, C.D. (1981). Some consequences of the Median self. *Journal of Symbolic Interaction*, *4*, 245–259.

Brown, B.W. (1980). Wife-employment, marital equality, and husband–wife violence. In M.A. Straus & G.T. Hotaling (Eds.). *The social causes of husband–wife violence* (pp. 176–187). Minneapolis: University of Minnesota Press.

Burke, P.J. (1980). The self: Measurement requirements from an interactionist perspective. *Social Psychology Quarterly*, *43*, 18–29.

Carlson, B.E. (1977). Battered women and their assailants. *Social Work*, *22*, 455–460.

Davidson, T. (1977). Wifebeating: A recurring phenomenon throughout history. In M. Roy (Ed.). *Battered women: A psychosociological study of domestic violence* (pp. 2–23). New York: Van Nostrand Reinhold Co.

Dellapa, F. (1977). Mediation and the community dispute center. In M. Roy (Ed.). *A psychosociological study of domestic violence* (pp. 239–249). New York: Van Nostrand Reinhold Co.

Denzin, N.K. (1984a). Toward a phenomenology of domestic, family violence. *American Journal of Sociology, 90,* 483–513.

Denzin, N.K. (1984b). *On understanding emotions.* San Francisco: Jossey-Bass Publishers.

Diener, E. (1979). Deindividuation, self-awareness, and disinhibition. *Journal of Personality and Social Psychology, 37,* 1160–1171.

Dobash, R.E., & Dobash, R.P. (1979). *Violence against women.* New York: Free Press.

Dollard, J., Doob, L.W., Miller, N.E., Mowrer, O.H., & Sears, R.R. (1939). *Frustration and aggression.* New Haven: Yale University Press.

Franks, D.D. (1985). Role-taking, social power and imperceptiveness. *Studies in Symbolic Interaction, 6,* 229–259.

Ganley, A.L. (1982). *Court-mandated counseling for men who batter: A three-day workshop for mental health professionals: Participant's manual.* Washington, DC: Center for Women Policy Studies.

Gelles, R.J. (1972). *The violent home: A study of physical aggression between husbands and wives.* Beverly Hills: Sage Publications.

Gelles R.J. (1985). Family violence. *Annual Review of Sociology, 11,* 347–367.

Gelles, R.J., & Straus, M.A. (1979). Determinants of violence in the family: Toward a theoretical integration. In W.R. Burr et al. (Eds.). *Contemporary theories about the family* (pp. 549–581). New York: Free Press.

Gingold, J. (1976). One of these days: Pow right in the kisser. *Ms., 5,* 51–54.

Goode, W.J. (1971). Force and violence in the family. *Journal of Marriage and the Family, 33,* 624–636.

Gorden, R.L. (1980). *Interviewing: Strategies, techniques, and tactics.* Homewood, IL: The Dorsey Press.

Gorden, S.L. (1981). The sociology of sentiments and emotions. In M. Rosenberg & R.H. Turner (Eds.). *Social psychology: Sociological perspectives.* New York: Basic Books.

Gorden S.L. (1987). Appropriating emotions to self from institutional and impulsive orientations. Working paper.

Hamberger, L.K., & Hastings, J.E. (1986). Personality traits of batterers—implications for treatment. Presented at the 1986 American Criminology Meetings.

Hochschild, A. (1979). Emotion work, feeling rules and social structure. *American Journal of Sociology, 85,* 551–575.

Hochschild, A. (1983). *The managed heart: Commercialization of human feeling.* Berkeley: University of California Press.

Hornung, C.A., McCullough, B.C., & Sugimonto, T. (1981). Status relationships in marriage: Risk factors in spouse abuse. *Journal of Marriage and the Family, 43,* 675–692.

Hull, J.G. (1981). A self-awareness model of the causes and effects of alcohol consumption. *Journal of Abnormal Psychology, 90,* 586–600.

Kemper, T.D. (1981). Social constructionist and positivist approaches to the sociology of emotions. *American Journal of Sociology, 87,* 337–362.

Kollock, P., Blumstein, P., & Schwartz, P. (1985). Sex and power in interaction. *American Sociological Review*, *50*, 34–46.

Langley, R., & Levy, R.C. (1977). *Wife beating: The silent crisis*. New York: Pocket Books.

Martin, D. (1976). *Battered wives*. New York: Pocket Books.

McCall, G.J., & Simmons, J.L. (1978). *Identities and interactions*. New York: The Free Press.

Mead, G.H. (1934). *Mind, self and society*. Chicago: University of Chicago Press.

Mead, G.H. (1938). *The philosophy of the act*. Chicago: University of Chicago Press.

Meltzer, B.N. (1978). *The social psychology of George Herbert Mead*. Kalamazoo, MI: Western Michigan University.

Mills, C.W. (1940). Situated actions and vocabularies of motive. *American Sociological Review*, *5*, 904–913.

Moore, D. (1979). *Battered women*. Beverly Hills: Sage Publications.

O'Brien, J.E. (1971). Violence in divorce prone families. *Journal of Marriage and the Family*, *33*, 692–698.

Pagelow, M.D. (1981). *Woman-battering: Victims and their experiences*. Beverly Hills: Sage Publications.

Perinbanayagam, R.S. (1977). The structure of motives. *Journal of Symbolic Interaction*, *1*, 104–120.

Pirog-Good, M.A., & Stets, J.E. (1986). Recidivism in programs for abusers. *Victimology: An International Journal*, *11*.

Pizzey, E. (1977). *Scream quietly or the neighbors will hear*. Short Hills, NJ: Ridley Enslow Publications.

Prentice-Dunn, S., & Rogers, R.W. (1982). Effects of public and private self-awareness on deindividuation and aggression. *Journal of Personality and Social Psychology*, *43*, 503–513.

Prescott, S., & Letko, C. (1977). Battered women: A social psychological perspective. In M. Roy (Ed.). *Battered women: A psychosociological study of domestic violence* (pp. 72–96). New York: Van Nostrand Reinhold Co.

Ptacek, J. (1985). Wifebeaters' accounts of their violence: Loss of control as excuse and as subjective experience. Unpublished paper, University of New Hampshire.

Rosenbaum, A. (1986). Of men, macho, and marital violence. *Journal of Family Violence*, *1*, 121–129.

Rosenberg, M. (1979). *Conceiving the self*. New York: Basic Books.

Roy, M. (1977). *Battered women: A psychosociological study of domestic violence*. New York: Van Nostrand Reinhold Co.

Roy, M. (1982). Four thousand partners in violence: A trend analysis. In M. Roy (Ed.). *The abusive partner: An analysis of domestic battering* (pp. 17–35). New York: Van Nostrand Reinhold Co.

Schuyler, M. (1976). Battered wives: An emerging social problem. *Social Work*, *2*, 488–491.

Scott, M., & Lyman, S. (1968). Accounts. *American Sociological Review*, *33*, 46–62.

Shott, S. (1979). Emotion and social life: A symbolic interactionist analysis. *American Journal of Sociology*, *84*, 1317–1426.

Stacey, W., & Shupe, A. (1983). *The family secret: Domestic violence in America*. Boston: Beacon Press.

Star, B. (1978). Comparing battered and non-battered women. *Victimology: An International Journal, 3*, 32–44.

Stearns, C.Z., & Stearns, P.N. (1986). *Anger: The struggles for emotional control in America's history*. Chicago: University of Chicago Press.

Steinmetz, S.K. (1978). The battered husband syndrome. *Victimology: An International Journal, 2*, 499–509.

Steinmetz, S.K. (1978). Violence between family members. *Marriage and Family Review, 1*, 2–16.

Stets, J.E., & Pirog-Good, M.A. (1987). Violence in dating relationships. *Social Psychology Quarterly, 50*, 237–246.

Straus, M.A. (1977). A sociological perspective on the prevention and treatment of wifebeating. In M. Roy (Ed.). *Battered women: A psychosociological study of domestic violence* (pp. 194–238). New York: Van Nostrand Reinhold Co.

Straus, M.A. (1979). Measuring intrafamily conflict and violence: The conflict tactics (CT) scales. *Journal of Marriage and the Family, 41*, 75–88.

Straus, M.A., & Gelles, R.J. (1986). Societal changes and change in family violence from 1975 to 1985 as revealed by two national surveys. *Journal of Marriage and the Family, 48*, 465–479.

Straus, M.A., Gelles, R.J., & Steinmetz, S. (1980). *Behind closed doors: Violence in the American family*. Garden City, NY: Anchor.

Stryker, S. (1980). *Symbolic interactionism: A social structural version*. Menlo Park: Benjamin Cummings.

Szinovacz, M.E. (1983). Using couple data as a methological tool: The case of marital violence. *Journal of Marriage and the Family, 45*, 633–644.

Tavris, C. (1982). *Anger: The misunderstood emotion*. New York: Simon and Schuster.

Turner, R.H. (1969). Role-taking: Process versus conformity. In A.R. Lindesmith (Ed.). *Readings in Social Psychology* (pp. 215–230). New York: Holt, Rinehart and Winston.

Turner, R.H. (1976). The real self: From institution to impulse. *American Journal of Sociology, 81*, 989–1016.

Walker, L.E. (1979). *The battered woman*. New York: Harper & Row.

Walker, L.E. (1979). How battering happens and how to stop it. In D. Moore (Ed.). *Battered women* (pp. 59–78). Beverly Hills: Sage Publications.

Whitehurst, R.N. (1974). Violence in husband–wife interaction. In S.K. Steinmetz & M.A. Straus (Eds.). *Violence in the family* (pp. 75–82). New York: Dodd, Mead and Co.

Wiley, N. (1979). Notes on self genesis: From me to we to I. *Studies in Symbolic Interaction, 2*, 87–105.

Author Index

Subject Index

Act,
    stages of the, 69–70, 116–117, 122–123, 129
    more than one, 93–95, 100, 157–158

Behavior,
    controlling, 111, 113–115, 120, 123

Contextual cues, 70–72, 83, 91, 95–99
Control,
    absence of, 155–156
    challenging the right to, 105–106, 123–126, 134
    external reference to, 71, 101, 119–120
    internal reference to, 71, 101, 119–120
    losing, 106–107, 123
    man's reference to, 65–66, 81–82, 119, 124–126
    regaining, 106–109, 123
    woman's reference to, 65–66, 81–82, 124–126
Control and violence,
    implications of, 127–132
Control as object, 18–19, 78, 101–102, 119, 121, 132
Controlling the woman, 1, 76, 101–103, 105, 111, 116, 120, 123, 125, 128, 130, 133–134,
Couple data, 1, 6–7

Domestic violence,
    class and, 3–5
    cycle of, 4, 6, 102
    definition of, 1
    factors associated with, 4–6
    feminism and, 3, 134
    forms of, 3
    generational theory of, 5
    history of, 2–3
    myths of, 4
    review of, 3–6
    staying in, 6
    theoretical approaches to, 9–11

Emotions, 57–61
    controlling, 111–113, 120, 123
    managing, 58–59, 68

Guilt, 74, 81, 83, 99, 103, 108, 129

"I," 11, 69–70, 72–77, 120, 122–123, 129–130
Identity, 8, 19, 132
Impulse to be violent,
    carrying out the, 74–77, 79, 83, 90–95, 99, 120, 122, 126, 130, 158
    checking the, 74–77, 79, 81, 83, 87–90, 99, 120, 122, 126, 129, 130
    inhibiting the, 74–77, 79, 83, 90–95, 99, 120, 122, 126, 130, 158